NEAR OCCASIONS
OF GRACE

Richard Rohr

ORBIS BOOKS

Maryknoll, New York 10545

The Catholic Foreign Mission Society of America (Maryknoll) recruits and trains people for overseas missionary service. Through Orbis Books, Maryknoll aims to foster the international dialogue that is essential to mission. The books published, however, reflect the opinions of their authors and are not meant to represent the official position of the society.

Published by Orbis Books, Maryknoll, NY 10545

This book has been adapted from previously published articles. Thanks are due to the following journals for permission to reprint material: *Sojourners* magazine for "Why Does Psychology Always Win?," "The Holiness of Human Sexuality," "An Appetite for Wholeness," "Reflections on Marriage and Celibacy," "Building Family," "All of Life Together Is a Stage," "Authors of Life Together," "A Life Pure and Simple," "To Be Jesus Resurrected," "The Energy of Promise," and "Baptism of Joy"; *Origins*, "Religious Life of the Future," a talk to the Conference of the Major Superiors of Men; *Radical Grace* for "Utterly Different and Exactly the Same" and "Naming Despair"; *Chariscenter USA* for "Risking Reconciliation: The Hope of Christian Unity"; *Praying* for "Out of a Prayerful Heart: An Interview with Richard Rohr" by Rich Heffern.

Manufactured in the United States of America

Library of Congress Cataloging-in-Publication Data

Rohr, Richard.
    Near occasions of grace / Richard Rohr.
        p.   cm.
    ISBN 0-88344-852-1
    1. Spirituality—Catholic Church.   2. Catholic Church—Doctrines.
I. Title.
BX2350.65.R64   1993
248.4'82—dc20   92-33193
                                                              CIP

To my Father, Richard Rohr, Sr., a man of the Kansas earth, a man of humility, a man of most generous spirit.

He made the heavenly Father believable and trustworthy, and freed me to love and imitate the good fathers of history, and to ignore the false patriarchs who will fall without my pushing.

By his life, "he pulled down the princes from their thrones and exalted the little ones." (Luke 1:52)

When grace is a punishment for you,
  you are in Hell.

When grace and punishment are fighting within you,
  you are in Purgatory.

When grace is received without payment or punishment,
  you are in Heaven.

CONTENTS

PREFACE

"The best things cannot be talked about," said Heinrich Zimmer. The second best things are usually misunderstood because we are using images and metaphors to point toward the first. So we spend most of our lives talking about the third best things because we need to talk and we long to be understood.

Risking misunderstanding, this book attempts to talk about the second best things, those qualities of life that always point beyond themselves to Something More. Many Christians grew up with warnings about avoiding "the near occasions of sin." In this collection of writings, which covers a period of fifteen years, Robert Ellsberg has patiently sifted through my thoughts on many pastoral issues and collected what we hope will be some *near occasions of grace* for believers and strugglers at the end of the second millennium of Christianity. We hope they will be such for you.

I do not think it is overly dramatic to say that Western civilization appears to be in a state of spiritual emergency; what is more surprising is that the church appears to be there too. For religion to be effective in linking us with the Something More, it must create a hopeful symbolic universe that both settles and liberates the human soul. The malaise of present-day Catholicism on both the right and left clearly reflects the fact that the Christ symbol is not being communicated to the Western soul. When "God reigns," the many disparate parts are held together in one coherent Totality, the Way-Things-Work is clear, even if demanding. But we no longer live in such a world. The cosmic egg has broken.

We are trying to preach the Gospel to people who are alien from their own roots and religious story. We must sadly describe ourselves as alienated at the core and foundation. Nothing else explains the massive neuroses of so many "normal" Western people who have secretly pledged allegiance to the wrong gods, while overtly saluting the flag of Christ. Schizophrenia, utterly split consciousness, is the tragic result.

In the practical order the result is polarization at every level. Groups are unable to respect one another, engage in civil dialogue, or basically honor what God is apparently patient about: the human struggle and the essentially tragic nature of all life. Ancient religion encoded such wisdom in pictures of wheels they called "inexorable." Eastern religion spoke of the yin and the yang of things. Catholic Christianity proclaimed it mythically and brilliantly as the Paschal Mystery: "Christ has died, Christ is risen, Christ will come again!" The Eucharistic ritual continues to name this pattern as *the* mystery of faith, but a people obsessed with progress, consumption, and the quick-fix no longer has the appropriate software to decode the message. The hardware, I believe, is still waiting in the vast unconscious near occasions of grace.

The rifts and chasms between good people today sometimes seem impossible to bridge. Let's just name a few obvious ones: male versus female, rich versus poor, liberal versus conservative, Christian versus non-Christian, "Pro-Choice" versus "Pro-Life," the overdeveloped world versus the underdeveloped world, renew-from-within versus change-from-without, straights versus gays, hierarchy versus laity, whites versus people of color—and every shade of every issue in between. We are all crowded on one limited planet and must somehow learn to live together while also maintaining the common earth beneath our five billion pairs of feet.

It is no one's fault in particular, but now it is our responsibility together to mend the breach. I cannot imagine what else would please and honor the Creator of us all. It is now somewhat of a waste of valuable time to try to impute blame on periods of history, nations, the church, or even our parents. When we no longer know how to constellate a symbolic universe, with God enthroned on the high altar, smaller loyalties on side altars, and gargoyles visible at the doors and corners of things, all we have left are private pathology and psychologisms to explain ourselves. Each group proclaims and protects its "rights," hurts, turf, and moral superiority to the other. A common life is no longer possible except in that small enclave of folks just like me. The "ek-klesia" of "called-out" people is no longer a promise of a new social order, but often a self-insured company invariably on the side of "protective ideas" which are too easily called holy and orthodox. While quite appropriate for the protection of the ego and the private self, such ideas very often have little to do with the daring and wonderful search for God. Mere credal or civil religion does not give us access to the rich and revelatory world of Spirit. In fact, it blocks the journey into grief, into the Mystery, into the Paradox, into the Great Unconscious, into ecstasy, into Universal Compassion, into the Cosmic Christ.

I believe that Jesus-who-became-the-Christ still stands as the perfect mediator of all that is human and good. The cross stands as the intersection of opposites between heaven and earth, divine and human, inner and outer — revealing at the same time the price of that intersection. It seems that the universal law is that something must always die for something else to live. It feels especially tragic and unacceptable when that something is not bad but good and seemingly necessary! It is the innocent Lamb that must be slain. Such is the "pattern that connects" all things, whether in the physical world, the world of animals and plants, the world of the psyche, or the world of relationships. But while the physical and animal worlds offer no resistance, this is not the case with human beings. In a quote that is probably difficult for self-important moderns to accept, C. S. Lewis insists that "we are not merely imperfect creatures who need to grow, but also rebels who need to lay down our arms." Perhaps the universal groaning of humanity and the earth will lead us to lay down our private weapons and pay the price of reconciliation in our lives and bodies. What else could be the message of the Paschal Lamb who is slain unto Life?

Because we are practical people, driven toward effectiveness, we look for a solution to our many problems. Perhaps a key is given in the very word "solutio" which in chemistry refers to the combination of *several* ingredients into a new mixture, each dying to its own substance. There is a natural resistance as I hold on to my exclusive story against a Larger Story. Usually we will not let go unless we are forced or wounded. In the mythologies of all the great world religions, the wounding is the passageway from the little world to the Transcendent World. The ego must be defeated before we will submit to the "solutio," before we will fit our small world into the Bigger Picture. If the wound leads us to this passing over, it is rightly called a sacred wound. If it leads me backwards to an entrenchment in my small protective ideas, the wound is the more common embittering wound. Here, I am afraid, is where much of the world and the church lies festering and bleeding, embittered that life has caused us pain.

Who will tell the world about the sacred wound? Who will announce the Kingdom on the other side of passing over? Who will show the children of God that they can trust the journey even now? Who will announce the wisdom and the mystery instead of just reiterating denominational boundaries and moral conclusions? Frankly, I think it will take ministers and healers of both sexes, ministers who are faithful somewhere while honoring God everywhere, ministers who are capable of universal table fellowship because they have stood faithfully in one place—which always means before One God. As Eugene Peterson said, we are waiting for those who are capable of a "long obedience in the same direction." That same direction may have as many curves and detours as a plate of spaghetti, but the soul knows to whom it has been obedient, and the Great Story tells it where it came from and where it is going. Our task is to continue to announce and live the sacredness of the wound. Our temptation is merely to pathologize, falsely celebrate, or create too-quick-order. Faith is our word for the staunch refusal to do any of the above. Without trust in God and a finally benevolent universe it is, of course, impossible to avoid taking control ourselves. It is impossible to trust the wounding and the defeat. But self-manufactured victories are transitory and offer no basis for real hope.

Spiritual emergencies are, however, undoubtedly occasions for spiritual breakthrough. And so in our time we live very near to the occasions of grace. The immensity of the pain and the immensity of the otherness are leading us to a necessary and new tryst with Life. We are seeing that there is nothing old under the sun, and the patterns of nature, Scripture, and other cultural mythologies are the true Orthodoxy. Most who call themselves traditionalists are not Traditional at all. They are just conservatives. And the ego is naturally conservative. Most liberals, on the other hand, cannot build anything that endures, because their final and true loyalty is to personal growth and political correctness. They refuse to accept the essentially tragic nature of life, the incoherent killing of the Innocent Lamb. It assaults every fibre of reason and order that the modern world has woven together. This book is *very Traditional*, and therefore some will call it radical. That is the pattern.

I will dare to talk of faith, myth, and mystery. I risk speaking of identity, boundaries, and the sacred. I even call Christians to a deep, personal, and *exclusive* commitment to Jesus, the Christ—precisely because his message is of a deep, personal, and *inclusive* commitment to all that God has created. A personal God leads us to a personalized and benevolent universe; a passionate God leads us and allows us to trust our own passion; a wounded God tells us that the absurdity and chaos are going somewhere. Jesus, the Cosmic Christ, is the pattern that connects, the Life that saves.

I pray that these second-best words will be near occasions of grace for you, my readers. I pray that my words will not get in the way of what God is doing in your lives and in the world. I pray that these words will not just be words, but "spirit and life" that plant you firmly in the breach between the world as it is (Power) and the world as it should be (Love). Both love and power are the necessary building blocks of God's Reign on this earth; both are to be respected and given their full due. For power without love is mere brutality (even in the church), and love without power is only the sentimentality of lives disconnected from the Whole. The Gospel in its fullness still holds the breach together, and is always my hope for the world. I draw strength from the words of Isaiah written after the exile:

> The ancient ruins will be rebuilt,
> You will build on age-old foundations,
> You will be called "Breach-Mender,"
> Restorer of ruined houses. (Isaiah 58:12)

If it takes exile to teach us such wisdom, then I welcome such exile. Only exiles are sufficiently torn from their kingdoms to mend and restore the "best things that cannot be talked about," the near occasions of grace that are always inviting us into Something More.

FR. RICHARD ROHR, O.F.M.
Center for Action and Contemplation
Albuquerque, New Mexico

NEAR OCCASIONS
OF GRACE

GOD'S GOOD NEWS

Meditations on Jesus

THE ENERGY OF PROMISE

Our age has come to expect satisfaction. We have grown up in an absolutely unique period when having and possessing and accomplishing have been real options. They have given us an illusion of fulfillment and an even more dangerous illusion that we have a right to expect fulfillment—and fulfillment now— as long as we are clever enough, quick enough, and pray or work hard enough for our goals.

We believe that we are energized by the bird in the hand; but believe it or not, the word of God and the history of those who have struggled with that word would seem to tell us that we are, in fact, energized much more by the bird in the bush. God's people are led forward by promises. It is promises, with all their daring and risk, that empower the hearts of people.

God's people are called through the enticement of the call itself, much more than through the direct vision of God's face, the certitude of God's answers, or the unfailing presence of God's joy. The Lord is "Our Justice" not by fulfilling us, but by calling us from where we are. God restores us not by making

1

it happen, but by promising us that it will. God tells us who we are by telling us who we are to become. Somehow that is enough. It works! At least it works for those who can learn how to believe: "Blessed is she who believed that the promises made to her would be fulfilled."

All wishful thinking to the contrary, it is not fulfillment which drives and calls and enriches humankind, but we are undoubtedly called forth by the mystery of what-could-yet-be. It is dreams that drive us and hopes that make us happen. And so God has given himself to us in a way that we could receive him and also benefit from him, even though we fail to see it as a gift or to praise him for the giving.

After all, they are just promises. And we believe only in the deed—now—in front of us. "Promises, promises!" has become a cynical and very understandable retort from a people who have grown tired of marketing lies and mere politics.

But God seems to have been around for a long time and does not take the momentary deed so seriously. God does not bother calling it the fulfillment of the promise. The Lord is apparently the Lord of the long haul. God has been making promises to David and Jeremiah, and promises to disciples for 2,000 years. To be absolutely honest I am not sure, from my very limited vantage point, that God has kept some of them to this day: Is David or even David's line "a just shoot"? Is Judah "safe"? Has Jerusalem ever really "dwelt secure"? Why did Jesus key up his contemporaries for some eschatological battles that we are still trying to get keyed up for?

The question is, precisely how does the Lord restore his people? How is "the Lord our Justice"? How does God make us, after initial creation, into ourselves?

I think we become like God by feeling with God; we become whole by becoming God's. I suspect that God knows the product pretty well. God knew that we would get sloppy through satiation. God knew that the numb would never notice and that the fulfilled would not feel. So our God has "tormented us with dissatisfaction" and only thrown us a few promises. But

they are enough to live on, and their deeds are the deeds of
the saints.

REMEMBERING THE FUTURE

How odd it is that God's salvation is so seldom recognized.
How strange that what God is offering is so rarely experienced.
We have presented salvation so poorly that much of the world
does not even take it seriously. Oh yes, we want help, we want
solace, we want magic, but I am not sure that we recognize or
even want the scary freedom that God calls salvation.

It is first of all a problem of seeing. We need to be taught
how to see. Just as an artist must learn again what she is seeing
in terms of edges, focus, perspective, colors and shadings, parts
and whole, so the believer must go back to the beginning and
start seeing anew. In order to see clearly the believer must
learn how to "remember": He or she must bring the pieces
back together again.

Memory is very often the key to understanding. Memory
integrates, reconciles, and puts the individual members into
perspective as a part of the whole. It seems that God has drawn
out love for us in a medium that we call time. For us to recognize what God is doing and therefore who God is, we must
pray like Paul "that your love may more and more abound, both
in understanding and wealth of experience." Love, in terms of
good will, is not enough. For love to happen effectively it must
be ordered and timed and cut to fit the receiver. I think this
is how God loves us! But we will never know it unless we remember.

Our remembrance that God has remembered us will be the
highway into the future, the straight path of the Lord promised
by John the Baptizer. Where there is no memory, there will be
no pain, but neither will there be hope. Memory is the basis
of both the pain and the rejoicing. We need to re-member both
of them; it seems that we cannot have one without the other.

Do not be too quick to "heal all of those memories," unless that means also feeling them deeply and taking them all into your salvation history. He seems to be calling us to suffer the whole of reality, to remember the good along with the bad. Perhaps that is the course of the journey toward new sight and new hope. Memory creates a readiness for salvation, an emptiness to receive love, and a fullness to enjoy it.

Strangely enough, it seems to be so much easier to remember the hurts, the failures, and the rejections. One almost wonders if we like the pain. We have grown comfortable with evil and have made friends with sin. And until we have learned how to see, it comes to us easily and holds us in its grasp. In a seeming love of freedom God has allowed us to be very vulnerable to evil.

Only in an experience and a remembering of the good do we have the power to stand against this death. As Baruch tells Jerusalem, you must "rejoice that you are remembered by God." In that remembrance we have new sight, and the evil can be absorbed and blotted out.

It takes a prophet of sorts, one who sees clearly, one who has traveled the highway before, one who remembers everything, to guide us beyond our blind, selective, and partial remembering: "Jerusalem, take off your robe of mourning and misery; put on the splendor of glory from God forever." Choose your friends carefully and listen to those who speak truth to you and help you remember all things, "so that you may value the things that really matter, up to the very day of Christ."

Ask the Lord for companions (sometimes Jesus alone!) who will walk the highway of remembering with you, filling in the valleys and leveling the mountains and hills, making the winding ways straight and the rough ways smooth. Then humankind shall see the salvation of God.

The repentance that the Baptist calls us to is one of remembering, and of remembering together, and then bearing the consequences of that remembrance. It is no easy matter, for the burden of re-membering is great. But we must try for the sake of truth, and we can try within the protective walls of church.

So "Up Jerusalem! Stand upon the heights; look to the east and see" your whole life. See what God has given freely. Your hope lies hidden in the past. "And rejoice that you are remembered by God."

WORD MADE FLESH

When God gives of himself, one of two things happens: either flesh is inspirited or spirit is enfleshed. It is really very clear. I am somewhat amazed that more have not recognized this simple pattern: God's will is incarnation. And against all of our godly expectations, it appears that for God, matter really matters.

This Creator of ours is patiently determined to put matter and spirit together, almost as if the one were not complete without the other. This Lord of life seems to desire a perfect but free unification between body and soul. So much so, in fact, that God appears to be willing to wait for the creatures to will and choose this unity themselves—or it does not even happen. (But if God did it any other way, the medium would not be the message.)

So the Lord apparently loves freedom as much as incarnation. And that is the rub of time and history and our interminable groanings. The sons and daughters of God waiting to appear are afraid of freedom and do not trust incarnation. So it took one who could say, "I have come to do your will, O God," to trust God's process instead of demanding God's conclusion. He is the perfectly incarnate Son. He is Jesus. Jesus trusted the process—"a body you have prepared for me." And so, like no other journeyman, he was totally ready for God's conclusion.

You see, there is a perfect continuum between the process and the conclusion, between incarnation and redemption, and between Jesus and those informed by the same Spirit of God.

The reason we have trouble with the full incarnation in Jesus is probably that we have not been able to recognize or admit our own limited incarnation. We also have a capacity for the divine. "For Christ plays in ten thousand places/Lovely in limbs, and lovely in eyes not his/To the Father through the features of men's faces"(Gerard Manley Hopkins, "As Kingfishers Catch Fire").

Theological doctrine we can deal with, but ourselves we cannot. It is comparatively easy to admit to a historical divine/human integration or personification, but it is apparently difficult to accept that same integration or personification within our own remembered and regretted lives. But this little self on its insignificant journey is very likely a microcosm of what God is doing everywhere and what God did perfectly in Jesus. If we are to believe the whole, we must start by trying to believe the part. If we are to love God's beginning and God's conclusion — Jesus — then we must try to love God's process — ourselves. He is Alpha and Omega, but we are beta, gamma, and delta. It is all one. Truth is one. And we have been made one by God's yes to flesh in Christ.

This mystery, this holy mystery, is so central that we must try to announce it in many and new ways. It is so filled with power that our reason and balance will resist and make compromises. Frankly, it is too much.

We, like Bethlehem, are too tiny to imagine greatness within us, but "you Bethlehem-Ephrathah, too small to be among the clans of Judah, from you shall come forth for me one who is to rule my people Israel." There is a whole to be found here, but it is only apparent as every part learns to love every other part. And I suspect that those who by grace can recognize the Lord within their own puny souls will be the same who will freely and intelligently affirm the Lord's presence in the body of Jesus and the body of the universe.

"But who am I that the Lord should come to me?" Elizabeth asks. Perhaps, if I can recognize and trust this little graciousness, this hidden wholeness, this child in the womb, then my spirit will be prepared for the greater visitation, the revelation of the Son of God. And yet we are always aware that God is not just an experience of mine, but more rightly, I am an experience in the mind and heart of God. This is very difficult for us self-centered moderns to comprehend. But if we dare to trust this holy mystery, we participate in a Presence that is at once overwhelming gift and precious surprise — not really demanded or necessary (at least, that is what we Franciscans say!) — but actually not difficult to believe at all!

So we Christians prepare to make festival, or as Thomas Merton puts it: "Make ready for the Christ, whose smile — like lightning — sets free the song of everlasting glory that now sleeps, in your paper flesh — like dynamite."

And God goes ahead enfleshing spirit and inspiriting the flesh; while for us, who have learned, like Elizabeth, to trust these holy visitations, our life leaps within us for joy!

TO BE JESUS RESURRECTED

The death of Jesus is either the end or it is the beginning. The Jesus journey either tells humankind that love is victorious and the risk is worth taking or it chronicles a sad and meaningless walk into despair. "If Christ has not been raised then our preaching is useless and your believing it is useless. . . . If our hope in Christ has been for this life only, we are the most unfortunate of all people" (1 Corinthians 15:15, 19).

Our faith is that the Father upheld the life of Jesus and reclaimed it as eternal. Jesus, therefore, is the really real. Or, to speak theologically, Jesus is eternal life. The resurrected Jesus is our assurance that it is okay to be human, even better to be noble, and best of all to be devoured for the sake of it.

Now as long as the cross in even its subtle forms is a scandal, then the resurrection is impossible to experience. Our faith is a choice against despair and against abandonment. Our hope is not just a hope for good fortune; it is a radical hope for God himself—that God is, in fact, who God should be—a love that we can understand.

To be true to himself and to his father's love, Jesus found himself undergoing both suffering and rejection. His pain was not just the pathetic and masochistic suffering and rejection of the sinful world, but it was precisely the result of his radical decision for the kingdom and kingdom values, which are "not of this world." In other words, Jesus was not an unfortunate victim of circumstances, but he in fact designed his own death by choosing for life "and life more abundantly." To opt for the really real is to find yourself at odds with most of the world's systems, institutions, expectations—and even religions. Jesus allowed that to happen in him—and the Father backed it up!

It is indeed difficult to lead people to believe in the "bad news" of the crucifixion. It is hard to trust death; ironically, it is even more difficult to trust the good news of resurrection. We are afraid to call upon the new power of risen life and expect it to be there. Or to put it another way, many Christians would sooner put up with death than confront it.

The resurrection of Jesus is an active assault upon the death and hopelessness of the world. Jesus stands in the midst of the fear of the upper room and turns it into Pentecost. To be Jesus Resurrected is to be a new power standing over and against the sick world. To be Jesus Resurrected is to be glorified body, new order, new world, new person; it is to be church. It seems that we cannot be the glorified body of Christ until we are first simply the body of Christ.

The good news of the resurrection is not that the poor victims of this world will finally triumph over the executioners, while the executioners will be fittingly punished. That is our petty notion of justification. It solves our momentary problems, but does not begin to reveal the love and glory of God. At that point God's love is not yet truly creative, new, or worthy of God. It is merely our finite projection.

If the resurrection is truly God's great answer and God's good news, then God is telling us that Jesus died and rose not only for the victims but also for the executioners. God is not just liberating the liberated and saving the saved. The new righteousness, the good news that is too good, is that God is somehow seeking to free the executioners too.

Alleluia! Alleluia!

2

CONVERSION

From Self-Actualization to Self-Transcendence

In growing psychologically, one moves toward increasing autonomy and independence. In growing spiritually, one increasingly realizes how utterly dependent one is, on God and on the grace of God that comes through other people.

Gerald May, *Will and Spirit*

The Age of Subjectivity

In the 1950s and '60s, there was an easy optimism afoot that touched the lives of most of us growing up. It was likely naive, partial, and uncritical, but it surely made human relating a bit easier. Things were what they seemed. Objectivity reigned, except among strange groups of bohemians who talked only to one another. Things were clear and distinct, we all liked Ike, and you just needed a good education to know what truth was and a good church to know who God was.

You did not need to know too much about yourself or your parents. Your unconscious was comfortably unconscious. If you followed the laws you were good and probably felt so; if you broke the laws you were bad, and church and state would remind you to feel bad. Now we know that most of the "laws" were products of the white, male system, but at least then we knew where we stood—and that offered a certain kind of real comfort to the psyche and to the society. I can see why the system lasted so long.

Let's call it the age of objectivity. Motivations, explanations, parental addictions were not the issue: God, simple belief systems, culture, and rituals held our lives together.

Then came subjectivity. A radical new reference point, a new jargon, a new truth, and a new level on which to interpret all human behavior. The psychological age began, and by the late 1960s it provided the language of the mainstream. It was a revolution just as profound and maybe more far-reaching than political revolutions or religious reformations of the past. All of us are deeply affected by it; it is the air we breathe.

The Jungian psychologist James Hillman summarizes it well:

> It's the prevailing opinion we encounter anywhere in the therapy world, the self-help world, the afternoon talk-show world. All make clear the importance of childhood, of coming out from disempowerment ("being in control"), recovering from past abuses, working through to self-acceptance ("I can be comfortable with that"), and the confessional witness of "my own journey." These advertisements for myself sound like the old Charles Atlas ads: "I was a ninety-seven-pound weakling, but look at me now."

Almost overnight the subjective self became objective truth. It was the unassailable "ground of being" which could not be questioned or left unaffirmed, at least in enlightened circles. One would sooner be caught theologically or politically incorrect than psychologically unaware or insensitive. The private self now had his or her character amor, and universities soon reported a dramatic drop in courses in philosophy, history, literature, foreign languages, and religious studies.

Our search for the permanent, the transpersonal, the civic, and the global was no longer much of a search. We had discovered personal existence, and questions of essence seemed boring. The "software" of things became so interesting that we began to ignore or even deny the hardware.

Now it was acceptable to seek life and growth in a largely verbal, mental, or conversational way. The best thing that one could do was "work on oneself." Adele Getty, a psychologist herself, says that "Rather than confront the social, political, and spiritual dilemma of the day, human growth has become a pacifier, the means to avoid the larger issues of human survival. Since society has 'no future' it makes sense to concentrate on one's own performance, and to practice transcendental self-importance." It may be acceptable to repress the objective issues of famine, destruction of habitat, medical care, and arms sales to everybody, but it is a mortal sin to repress any feelings, fears, or sexual fantasies.

The psychological and the subjective are bottomless and fascinating. You do not need to have a degree to enter into the conversation. In fact, a past experience of crime, abuse, or destructive behavior actually gives you authority. Psychological conversation provides both instant intimacy and a sense of control.

What we are seeing is an enormous confusion between what philosophers call *existence* and *essence*. We are attaching enormous significance to passing feelings, hurts, and experiences which the great world religions have variously termed illusion, temptation, trial, grace, opportunity, passion, or "shadow and disguise." They are means, not ends, windows and doorways perhaps, scaffolding to be discarded, but surely not the temple itself. Not the thing in itself.

In the classic traditions of Christian spirituality, the search for understanding or sobriety or healing is seen at best as the early "purgative way," but not yet the classic "illuminative" or "unitive" paths. In true spirituality and healthy religion, we are always pointed back and through ever-changing psyche to never-changing Spirit. But in the encounter between spirituality and psychology, it is my observation that psychology usually wins. It needn't be a choice of one or the other. In classic theology grace *always* builds on nature. It is just that nature today seems to be afraid there is no grace at all.

The Language of Individualism

The first and unquestioned language of American life is the language of individualism. Alexis de Tocqueville began speaking of this in his early study *Democracy in America*: "Such folks owe no [one] anything and hardly expect anything from anybody. They form the habit of thinking of themselves in isolation and imagine that their whole destiny is in their own hands."

In the psychological age, this first language has taken a new twist. Philosopher William Sullivan calls it the language of romantic expressionism. It is a private language of concern, sensitivity, and individual rights. No one in polite company can disagree with it without appearing to be a complete boor. It is warm, affectionate, and infinitely respectful of each person's feelings, hurts, and needs. To be PI (politically incorrect) in this area is to incur the wrath of otherwise tolerant liberals and broad-minded believers. Individual rights are the ultimate virtue; individual responsibility is seldom spoken of, lest "guilt" be incurred.

The language of romantic individualism subverts many other honest conversations with such phrases as "You must be true to yourself," "Listen to your feelings," and "I have a right to. . . . " No one can counter such comments, even though there is little philosophical ground for such assertions. Thus we must prepare ourselves for a future of endless debates about competing rights and bottomless struggles over competing feelings.

The psychological age has found a surprising and rather ingenious method of gaining power: Playing the victim. Given the language of romantic expressionism, no one can criticize you without appearing to be crass and politically incorrect. It's the ultimate and impregnable position. Every talk show is about people who are "outraged" and "offended" by some other group who want their particular totem protected and enthroned.

The talk show hosts become the public arbiters of victimhood. Oprah and Geraldo hear both sides, insults and injustices are dragged out, and the crowd decides who is the greater victim. Because there is no objective reference point, Madonna can end up looking like an abused, misunderstood innocent, and fathers who don't offer child support are seen as manipulated by their greedy wives.

To hurt, to suffer, to deserve sympathy is to have achieved moral victory. Once you can prove that you are indeed a victim, no more can be demanded of you than the perpetual right to tell your story. The rest of us must feel the appropriate guilt and offer propitiatory incense.

We all know that there are real victims, and the role of the prophet is to proclaim their story publicly. But sophisticated, psychological society has used the profound Christian archetype of the Lamb to gain negative power for people who are often merely bitter with their own vendetta. The victimhood of Jesus is a matter of accepting, forgiving, and non-self-serving. The Lamb of God takes away the sin of the world; the victim lambs insist that the rest of the world has sinned against them. The first redeems. The second deadens and paralyzes.

The Loss of Community

Many of us are aware of the failure of so many exciting attempts at community in the 1970s and the '80s. Many such communities died, I fear, because they talked, met, and worried themselves to death. After years of in-house and seemingly cyclical conversations, many movers and shakers decided to move on. Usually they later admitted that community was an excellent school of growth, character, and conversion. But it was too often not a "home."

When two or two hundred people all feel that they have the

right to demand full understanding, support (the sacred word), and partnership in their private pain, most folks soon find a more humane place to live. Salvation by interaction expects and often demands from other people what the objective tradition said only God could give.

"Save me," says the newcomer to community. Give me a secure and happy home here on Earth, be my mother and father in a nurturing (but not a restrictive) way. Yet we all know that you can only marry one person at a time, you cannot meet even most of his or her needs, and in the end you still remain a profound mystery to one another. I wonder if the great mystery of forgiveness is even possible without an acceptance of radical Mystery. I doubt it.

I see now why the Rule of St. Benedict and the Rule of St. Francis have stood the test of time. The boundaries are clear and the wheel does not need to be re-invented with each new personality that jumps in the buggy. Historic Christian community did not depend upon charisma, articulateness, or even understanding. The novices' "needs" were left unmet, until they discovered what they really desired. The community hoped it would be God, not human sympathy.

Claude Levi-Strauss says that myth in each culture teaches "the appropriate distance between things." Today we have no myths except modern romances. Such expectations of false and impossible intimacy will continue to make community in America very difficult, and sometimes even counterproductive. The thousands of disillusioned and alienated ex-community members are a judgment not only on the limitations of their communities but also on their own narcissistic expectations. Community cannot at once be re-parenting, adult education, home away from home, therapeutic society, and support group for our own private agendas.

If we look at the great myths of religious and secular history, we see that events, historical trials, and concrete circumstances are themselves the primary teachers. For the Jewish and Christian tradition, God is specifically encountered in history and relationships, and not in analysis. Community and commitments, and the trials thereof, help people grow up. Heroism has to do with character, but character shows itself in action and deed. In contrast, we have substituted personality for character, being for doing.

We are the first civilization that substitutes celebrities for true heroes and heroines. It is hard to think of a true hero who is idealized in our culture today. Now it is enough to be well-known for the sake of being well-known. The ten most admired Americans each year are typically those who have been most in the news. It is amazing—but surely also disastrous for the education of the next generation.

Being *without* doing becomes mere image and the management of image. The talk show, the self-help book, psychobabble—these are now allowed to replace direct learning, responsible action, and civic virtue. Being *with* doing teaches us that life is hard, we don't and shouldn't always get our own way, and success has many surprising faces.

We must recognize that a life of mere interiority and discussion is a luxury for the rich. Considering the state of humanity and the planet, this is not the time to "create your own reality." This New Age shibboleth is symptomatic of a pattern of fear and denial that recognizes the decline of the American Empire, but has no alternative in which to believe. And believers are still hesitant to live the public reality: "The kingdom of God is not a matter of talk but of power" (1 Corinthians 4:20).

In the past, work, religion, and citizenship were the classic entry ways into the public life of doing. It is these three that have been coopted by the private and psychological mind. Work is no longer vocation, but a minimal occupation to put bread on the table. Religion in middle-class society thrives on therapeutic and trendy jargon. And citizenship has shattered into small special-interest groups, if it exists at all.

Where is the person who will model for us the beauty of

political holiness? Where are the contemplative activists? I will race to their doorways.

Knowing and Loving

I have always found an unsolvable paradox in the Genesis account of the Fall. Why did Yahweh tell Adam that he could "eat of all of the trees in the garden, but of the tree of the knowledge of good and evil you are not to eat, for on the day you eat of it you will most surely die" (Genesis 2:16-17)? Why would the great temptation and the great sin involve doing something that appears to be necessary and healthy? "The woman saw that the tree was good to eat and pleasing to the eye, and that it was desirable for the knowledge that it could give" (Genesis 3:6). I think God is trying to reveal an obvious but not always obvious truth: Loving is not about knowing.

This confusion was present in the religious literati who justified the death of Jesus. Later it showed itself in the heresies of Pelagianism and Gnosticism (we can be saved by correct effort or correct knowledge!). The medieval church became masterful at casuistry and mystification of the clear teaching of Jesus. The Enlightenment told us, "I think, therefore I am." Even the Reformation had much more to do with theology than praxis.

Now we seek salvation by interaction and theory—all understandable attempts to eat of the tree of knowledge of good and evil. *Knowing* becomes an excuse, a delay, a salt substitute for that surrender to Love, which is "always ready to excuse, to trust, to hope, and to endure whatever comes" (1 Corinthians 13:7).

Let's admit that this freedom (the only freedom the gospel promises us) is almost lost in our time, even in the churches. Everything must be managed, understood, explained, talked through, worked out, confronted, and exposed (except social injustice). In such a private, heady, and protective world, love has a hard time breaking through. We "understand all the mysteries there are, and know everything, and have faith in all its fullness to move mountains, but [are too often] without love" (1 Corinthians 13:2). But religion, spirituality, the search for God are not about knowing; they are *always* about love.

I have no desire to be reductionist, anti-intellectual, or make naive claims that "love conquers all." I would like to deal with the objective phenomena that most of our communities have died amid tons of expertise, that far too many projects and programs crash on the rocks of hurt feelings, and that pressing issues we all want to deal with usually flounder on in-house issues of ego, power, and personality conflicts.

I've heard that 80 percent of ministry today is taken up with personnel and grievance work with staff. Is this what it might mean to be banished from the primal garden? Are these "the cherubs with flaming swords guarding the return to the tree of life" (Genesis 3:24)? We have surely died by eating so voraciously from this tree. Many other parts of human existence, including shared memory, the patience of space and time, the holy realm of mystery and symbol and myth, have all been repressed in favor of a knowing that really means controlling.

Jesus found the way back to the garden, ironically, by going into the desert. It is no accident that this is the very first act he performs after his baptism. There he cleans the lens, empties the false self, and faces directly the illusions of effectiveness, rightness, and control (the three temptations in Matthew's gospel), finally shouting at Satan, " 'You must worship the Lord your God, and serve God alone.' And at that the devil left him" (Matthew 4:10-11).

I wonder if there is any less radical way to get back to our essence. In the desert Jesus mandated the absolute pivot from an anthropocentric worldview to a theocentric one. Without the desert, religion is largely the maintenance of self-image, and psychology is its newest toy.

Contemplation

Contemplation is a way to describe what Jesus did in the desert. It's not learning as much as it is unlearning. It's not explaining as much as containing and receiving everything, and holding onto nothing. It's refusing to judge too quickly and refining quietly in observation and awareness.

You cannot understand things once you have approved or disapproved. There is too much *you* there! Contemplation is loosening our attachment to ourselves so that Reality can get at us, especially the Absolute Reality that we call God. William McNamara rightly calls contemplation "a long loving look at the Real." Aldous Huxley calls it "the perennial philosophy."

Contemplation is the most radical form of self-abandonment that I can imagine. It is most difficult if there is not a profound trust that there is Someone to whom I can be abandoned. Such self-forgetfulness, paradoxically, leads one to a firm and some-what fearless sense of responsibility. Now I can risk responsibility precisely because I know the buck does not stop here. There is a co-creation going on, a synergism between surrender and personal responsibility, God "co-operating with those who love God" (Romans 8:28).

As such, contemplation is most difficult and even unnatural in an overstimulated world of images and attachments to them. It is next to impossible as long as we identify with our passing feelings and opinions. For that very reason we have made it the *sine qua non* of our "school for prophets" at the Center for Action and Contemplation. No new perception, no new engagement, no honest name for God will emerge in our cluttered existence apart from a contemplative stance which relativizes mere psychological data.

The psychological mind assumes that a society can hold together without any "story" that is commonly held to be true. All we need to do is pursue the freedom and self-actualization of each member. The modern liberal type believes that this is sufficient to give a people meaning and coherence.

I am convinced that much if not most, of the modern neurosis is a direct result of the lack of a common, shared story under which our individual stories are written. As a result, our tiny lives lack a transcendent referent, a larger significance, a universal and shared meaning. Our common life is a "dis-aster," literally disconnected to the cosmic "stars." We are lost in insignificance.

Long after the centuries of fighting over the humanity and the divinity of Christ, the Western church has gradually lost touch with the larger and more universal message: "The image of the unseen God, the firstborn of all creation, for in him all things were created in heaven and on earth . . . through him and for him . . . and he holds all things in unity . . . because God wanted all perfection to be found in him and all things to be reconciled through him and for him" (Colossians 1:15-20).

This is not a problem-solving Christ, not a denominational or cultural Christ, not a Christ domesticated by the churches, but the One who names in his life and person what *matters*, what *lasts*, and finally what *is*. He holds it all together in significance, reveals the redemptive pattern that we call the life and death of things, and holds the meaning and value of our lives *outside of ourselves*!

Because we no longer "worship" such a Christ, we are condemned to worship smaller gods, and to build our lives around smaller stories. We try to replace him with colorized myths of pilgrims, George Washington, and Norman Schwarzkopf, but none of them are big enough or real enough to give universal order and meaning. We look to the private psyche but it is just not big enough or connected enough to encompass human spiritual longing.

The Christian church's efforts at evangelization will remain trapped in culture and fundamentalism until we are ourselves large enough to proclaim a Cosmic Christ. I am sure the psychological age is insufficient to the task. As James Hillman has said of his own profession, "Psychological counseling literalizes problems, and by killing the possibility of seeing through to their madness, kills the spirit."

We are killing the Spirit, I believe, in a new and still surprising way. Not by legalism but by psychological correctness, not by knowing but by refusing not to know, not by omission but by a managing-fixing-explaining of life that is a new and acceptable disguise for control, not by authoritarian leadership but by individuals who respect no authority except their private experience. This diminution of life calls into question almost all of the religious and spiritual traditions of the world religions. Further, it limits enlightenment to those who are educated, articulate, leisure class, and well-funded.

I claim the longer Tradition. I trust older guides, without rejecting the new. I remember the words of the monk Thomas Merton: "Faith, patience, and obedience are the only guides that help us advance quietly in darkness without looking at ourselves."

3

PURE PASSION

The Holiness of Human Sexuality

EMBODIED SPIRIT

Human sexuality has been so long denied a hearing that it remains in a shadowlike world and is seldom retrieved in a positive and creative way. Such a powerful aura surrounds the subject, which is both terribly attractive and wonderfully frightening, that I am quite sure we are dealing with a dimension of holiness.

Both the Holy One and the Evil One know something that we are only beginning to suspect: power has been hidden in weakness, "mystery has been masked as a mistake." God knew that only humble vulnerability could be entrusted with spiritual power—and so God hid it like a treasure in the body of Jesus (Ephesians 3:5, 9; 1 Corinthians 2:7, 10; Colossians 1:26). "My power is at its best in weakness," Paul tells us. "For it is when I am weak that I am strong" (2 Corinthians 12:9-10). "And what is more, it is precisely the parts of the body that seem to be the weakest which are the indispensable ones" (1 Corinthians 12:22). Why? "So that the sovereignties and powers should learn only now, through the church, how comprehensive God's wisdom really is" (Ephesians 3:10).

We are only now daring to believe, after 2,000 years of revelation of the mystery of Christ, what Satan discovered at the crucifixion. The Evil One knows that the place to attack us is in the area where we are most subject to shame, where we are most weak and truly "out of character": our bodiliness. Satan knows that is the last place where we will expect or look for God. And God knows that only forgiven sinners and spiritual searchers will find God there.

So Evil has found the breach in the wall and attacked each one of us there with "a thorn in the flesh, an angel of Satan" (2 Corinthians 12:7). And unfortunately, it has worked! Much of the tradition has been negatively and uselessly trapped in guilt and preoccupation with the flesh, while the great issues of gospel and grace have gone unheeded. The result has been rigidity and repression—much of it called "holiness." This response has been Evil's greatest triumph over gospel freedom. It has horribly entrapped the positive power of human affection, which is the heart of the matter.

But the embodied and hidden Christ is still coming forward in history, "a mystery hidden for generations and centuries and revealed to his saints. It was God's purpose to reveal it to them and to show all the rich glory of this mystery to pagans. The mystery is Christ among you, your hope of glory" (Colossians 1:26-27). This Christ will have his harvest, and it will be through weak flesh, that least-suspected place, that health and growth will be revealed.

We must begin, however, with a firm act of trust in what God has done in Jesus. We cannot return to a healthy Jewish and incarnational view of reality until we accept that God has forever made human flesh the privileged place of the divine encounter. We have had enough of dualism, enough of mystification, and enough of gnosticism. We must reclaim the incarnation as the beginning point of the Christian experience of God. We must return to the Hebrew respect for this world and for ourselves. This is the mind that formed Jesus. He freely became body, and I am body. It is the only self that I have ever known. We have no other beginning point, we have no other receiver station—except this body-person that God has created and apparently trusted and named "temple."

What God has trusted, I am going to start trusting. What God has been willing to release and take risks with, I must also risk. After more than twenty years of retreat work and spiritual direction, I am convinced it is the only way of wisdom, and is not the way of laxity and decadence that so many fear. Teilhard de Chardin, the French scientist-poet-priest, put it perhaps best of all: "Avoiding the risk of a transgression has become more important to us than carrying a difficult position for God. And it is this that is killing us."

Only when someone gives us permission to start trusting ourselves do we also start listening to ourselves, do we take ourselves seriously, as I believe God does. Only when we start trusting ourselves do we also begin to take responsibility for ourselves and for our mistakes. Only then do we grow and become "fully mature with the fullness of Christ himself" (Ephesians 4:13). In this transient world of human limitation, there is nothing purely secular or purely sacred. There is only good direction and bad direction. Jesus came to show us the way—the way through. The theologians call it the "Paschal Mystery," the way of dying and rising.

We must admit that both directions are happening in our lives, and it is in this creative tension that the spiritual journey finds its energy and force. All else is illusion. The wondrous work of grace is to be able to gather those opposing forces together in one place and make them into forces for life rather than death. We call it holiness.

I am sure that bodies have been literally entangling themselves with one another since the beginning of time. It is rather basic and universal and not really that surprising when you consider that this "who" that we are appears to be encased in a bodily sheath. We seem to like, or even need, to be touched, to be reminded that we are alive or that we matter to another. Most so-called "primitives" seem to be naturally aware of this, whereas most products of civilization have created huge denial systems and taboos to protect themselves from its power. As you might expect, the need only takes on more sophisticated and subtle disguises, and we have a sexuality we no longer understand or have any creative control over.

Superficial observation would tell us that bodies are trying to express themselves to one another, bodies are trying to feel good, bodies are trying to unite with one another, bodies are trying to overcome the pain, bodies are enslaved to their own chemical and hormonal needs, bodies are trapped in being body. Frankly, I cannot deny that many if not most bodies are entrapped. I would agree with the most rigid moralists that something is awry here. But if we are to exorcise this demon of sensuality or lust, we must first name the demon rightly. We must know what is really happening, or we might call forth the wrong demon and deny the right angel.

It appears to me that bodies are not so much trapped in being body as they are feverishly trying to become spirit. They are not so much trying to express themselves as they are trying to become themselves. They are not so much trying to become one with another body as they are trying to become one within themselves. Bodies are not nearly so preoccupied with union between the opposing sexual polarities as desperately seeking union within their own sexual selves. In all truth, many bodies are not so much seeking to overcome the pain as to deeply and definitely feel the pain of being alone and human. Sexuality is much more a journey into the inner darkness than a denial of it. Even the anguished looks and suffering groans of lovers reveal the truth that our unconscious has grasped hold of: I am still alone.

Yet the opposite is also true. A person who has been allowed to grow, make mistakes, trust him- or herself, change, and grow again into other mistakes and graces will probably experience the profound nature of human and divine communion. And once that is experienced, mere genital sex is forever relativized and revealed for the avenue and window that it is. These people will be capable of deeper and deeper communion and yet not become enslaved to its momentary rituals. This must be what we mean by gospel freedom.

We must admit that the Christian tradition has been largely blinded by this aspect of freedom. If there is such a thing as a corporate Christian shadow, an area of life that has been denied existence, it is surely in this area of the positive character of human sexuality. How ironic that the very religion that has believed that God became flesh has been the most consistently negative in its relatedness to human flesh.

How did we come to this point? In the New Testament period there were already elements of Stoicism present. Then we moved into various forms of dualism. Monastic and hermetical asceticism took the place of an idealized martyrdom for Christ; penance and mortification were often sought for their own sake in many religious communities; the medieval church found itself preoccupied with death, purgatory, and fear of hell. The questions of the Reformers were largely concerned with church structures and theological definitions, but not with the corporal works of mercy or the quality of human life. And we then continue with 400 years of "angelism," Pietism, Puritanism, Victorianism, and endless Catholic legalism and Protestant verbalism. Furthermore, we export it in good colonial fashion to all the corners of the earth in the name of Jesus.

"No!" is not wisdom. And now in our time we are reaping the rewards of such repression. Much of the Western world has given up on the church and is going other places for wisdom. Unfortunately, in these other places they are sometimes "willingly filling their belly with the husks the pigs are eating" (Luke 15:16). But we in the church must ask ourselves if we have not been the parent who sent them away because there was nothing trustworthy or life-giving at home.

We must face up to our past bias against emotions, our condescending attitude toward the body, and our love/hate relationship with our genital-sexual selves. If we are to be honest, we must admit that the tradition has always been gnostic, overly spiritual and "metaphysical." It has preferred to struggle philosophically with abstract theological questions. It divided peoples, churches, and history over discussions of the relationship of the Spirit to the Father and the Son, the relationship of the divine and human natures of Christ ("hypostatic union"). It gave rigid, reasoned solutions to biblical promises of God's presence ("transubstantiation") and salvation (theories of "justification" and "atonement"). The Western church has been afraid of the wholistic intuitions of our deepest selves for centuries now, and has lost the power of synthesis and the energy of paradox. In that sense, it has surely lost touch with its biblical roots and the transformative power of the Judeo-Christian religion.

I do not believe that any of these questions were or are idle or unimportant. But the trouble is that we never saw them as anything more than theological. It might have been more fruitful for the human race if we had drawn out the implications of the hypostatic union for our own lives instead of simply affirming it as a theological datum. We never connected the truth of our questions to real life. We were more concerned with spiritual control than we were with spiritual power. And our fear of spiritual power has put us out of touch with the spiritual world in general and the sexual world in particular.

Perhaps this proves the point that theology is best done by those who are also in practical and pastoral ministry. For after centuries we have not been able to put human and divine, flesh and spirit together in any believable and creative way. And now Western civilization finds itself in a largely decadent sexual rebellion, with an inability to creatively use and understand its emotional life, and with an exaggerated idolization of materiality, precisely, I believe, because the Western church has failed to give the world what God gave the world in Jesus — incarnation (John 1:1-18) and integration (Colossians 1:15-20).

Let's go one step further in our attempt to name this demon. I think all of the above is understandable for any number of historical and cultural reasons. The church has been the victim

of history as much as it has been the creator of it. It seems
that God is humble enough to put up with that and wait for
maturation. But the problem is deeper. I think we could deal
with a church that is human, secular, and caught up in bodiliness and emotion. In fact, I think that would even be a reform.

But what makes the situation most difficult and elusive is
that since its beginnings the church has been grossly material
and engaged in the physical while pretending that it is not. It
continues to use the language of abstraction and mystification,
so that no one does know, is able to know, or should even want
to know what this refers to in the world of human experience.
Christianity refuses to admit that it is historical and human. It
refuses to recognize that it moves in the vehicle of culture, and
so it becomes trapped in culture, all the while using the language of counterculture, almost as if it is trying to fool itself.

Note, for example, the early cult of relics and shrines, the
continuing "edifice complex" of the Western church, the preoccupation, sometimes bordering on obsession, with sexual
morality, the temporal power struggles of the papacy, the self-
serving ritualism of many Orthodox groups, the behavioristic
and cultural morality of much of Protestantism. All of these
could be seen as the physical entrapments of a Christianity that
refuses to admit that it is human and historical. It is a victim
of what it denies in its idealized self. It has shown itself very
weak in the true discernment of spirits, often incapable of dis-
tinguishing true good from real evil. As a result, it is not really
at home in what should be its eminent domain: spirituality and
its bodily manifestation, sexuality. It has not yet developed the
eyes to see that some of what it considers to be its greatest
assets might well be its liabilities, and some of what it considers
to be its weaknesses might well be its greatest strengths.

We thought we could deal with God on paper and meet God
in correct practice, whereas the biblical pattern seems to be
that we can meet God only in our own history and precisely as
we face our own sinfulness. We thought that when we had
condemned monophysitism (the belief that Jesus is one nature,

fully divine and not human) on paper as a heresy we had dealt with it. In fact, the church has been not only gnostic for much of its history but also monophysite. Fortunately, there have been graced breakthroughs in the lives of whole and holy men and women, and momentary syntheses. Unfortunately, it seems that what you deny and repress is, in fact, what controls and forms you. We have refused to dialogue, listen to, accept, and relate to our sexuality positively. Now we find ourselves awkward and out of touch with its positive meaning. It haunts us from its shadowed position.

Our direction, of course, is to go back to the beginning and perhaps to "know the place for the first time" (T. S. Eliot). Christ, "the Flesh-taker" will be our guide. "Before anything was created, he existed, and he holds all things together in unity. God wanted all fullness to be found in him, and all things to be reconciled through him and for him, everything in heaven and everything on earth" (Colossians 1:17, 19).

In Jesus we see God as the "perfect exchanger," to use Rosemary Haughton's apt image of the trinitarian God. He gives only what he has first received (John 5:19, 8:28), and he holds back nothing that God has given to him (John 15:15); he becomes the perfect receiver and therefore the perfect giver: "For the Father, who is the source of life, has made the Son the source of life" (John 5:26).

The New Testament language for God is not so much sexist or concerned with dominance or pre-eminence as it is with the essential character of whole relationship. The Spirit is the personal and personalizing result of such vulnerable exchange. Sin is the refusal to exchange—either to receive or to give back. Sin is to claim the self as an independent possession or as a private right. Sin is always a type of self-absorption, which is a lie about the nature of reality; whereas the Spirit, who teaches all truth, celebrates and reconciles that which is fragmented. The Spirit of God makes all things one by reminding them that they are first one—more one than many fragmented parts of a larger whole.

What looks like discovery is really recognition. What appears to be exploration is much more homecoming. The Spirit unites. Sin always separates. The work of God is total and full reconciliation. In other words, our only real badness consists in the repression of our goodness, which is the Spirit given and promised. And that is indeed bad.

Empirically, this badness shows itself in hardness, closedness, non-listening, the refusal to feel, self-hatred in its many disguises, and superficiality in general. This is the great sin of non-belief, which aborts the human soul a thousand times a day. We refuse to believe in what the Son has told us we are — sons and daughters of the living God. We hate ourselves mercilessly, and in many ways our preoccupation with sins has kept us from the recognition of this great sin. It is the unforgivable and unrecognized sin against the Holy Spirit. Unforgivable because it is unrecognized disbelief in what God has done.

It is here that the Christian tradition opens us to true wisdom. First, it has defined God as "Trinity," or vulnerability, communion, and mutuality. No other religion, therefore, provides such a beginning and basis for a theology of relationship. The Christian God is not a loner. The Christian God is perfect right relatedness.

Secondly, therefore, the Judeo-Christian tradition reveals a God who is passion. God is not the passionless and omnipotent abstraction of the philosophers, although we have often tried to make it seem so. God is angry, tender, jealous, and seems to be hopelessly in love. God is so "out of control" with this love that he makes unilateral promises and covenants that we cannot break or change. God is apparently willing to wait around for centuries for a believing response, and puts up with all kinds of abuse in the meantime. A real fool, of sorts.

But that is what passion does to you: it makes you feel and it makes you suffer — so much so that we use the same word for both meanings. As you might expect, we are not quite sure whether we want a God with passion. We have not yet learned how to live with that reality. But God seems to be here to stay, and I think that will finally make all the difference. God is not going to change. But we will, I'm sure. We cannot resist God's passion for us much longer.

Which brings us to the third enduring value of the tradition: faithfulness. It has almost taken us this long to realize that time itself is the great revelation. "Staying in there" gives us the time in which to see the patterns and rhythms of life and love.

If we listen, if we keep listening, we will know. If we remember, and we keep remembering, we will meet. If we are willing to go deep in at least one place, we will recognize continuities, direction, and purposefulness. We will say, "Who is upholding me?" "Who is this being good to me?" "Is there someone walking with me, or ahead of me?" Then we will meet the Faithful One. And then faithfulness will make sense. In fact, it will be the only thing that will make sense out of anything. Faithfulness is the pattern of God. "Staying in there" is the sign of salvation.

Fourthly, the Jewish tradition in particular makes us aware of the constant danger and nature of idolatry. It teaches us that we are habitually addicted to the making of gods. We are fascinated with absolutes and answers. We are terrified by ambiguities and paradox. We want a "rightness" that we can always rely upon, a power that is always in control and on our side. We want a warm body that will protect us from our own coldness. We want almost anything rather than journey, and search, and trial and error. So we make gods that do not last, and "their makers end up like them" (Psalm 135:18).

The tradition tells us, however, that all human and created things are to be relativized and put in harmonious balance. This includes our relatedness to and expectations of others, our sexual taboos, our bodily pleasures, and even our individual rights to happiness. As old-fashioned as that sounds, I think that is what the Scriptures are saying. As someone once said, conservatives are not necessarily wrong about their certitudes. It is just that they are too easily certain about too much. That form of conservatism creates a lot of idols for all of us and keeps us from religious surrender.

In this area of sexuality we all seem to have our areas of blindness and our sacred cows that cannot be touched. The liberals will find some way to say that it is always good, the conservatives are determined to enforce the law. Both seem to be nervous about nuance. Idols, with clear shape and explanation, seem to be easier to live with. The wisdom from the tradition, therefore, is that whatever God is doing, it is certainly beyond cultural fears, fads, and social taboos. This is particularly true in this area where there has been so much overlapping, and where it is most difficult to distinguish what God is really saying from "what my mother told me," and from what my mother church told me. Only the tradition gives us the criteria for individual and wise discernment.

I think that the tradition has handed on to open and obedient people a very intuitive and almost common-sense wisdom about what is real and what is unreal in regard to our sexual relatedness. It gives us an arena in which to move and discover our true bodily and spiritual selves.

The Catholic Theological Society's study *Human Sexuality* (Doubleday, 1979) summarized it rather well when it stated that our sexual actions must aim to be "self-liberating, other-enriching, honest, faithful, socially responsible, life-serving, and joyous." That is certainly the task and journey of a lifetime, but it is no more or no less than what Jesus said when he taught the greatest commandment of love of God and love of neighbor. The two loves "resemble" (Matthew 22:39) one another. They are each the school of the other. We will learn how to be properly sexual as we understand the properly passionate relationship that God has with us. And we will learn how to be properly spiritual as we come to understand the true character of human longing and affection.

Finally, the only biblical mandate that matters is to copy and allow the pattern of God's love in us. If this sounds soft and liberal, perhaps it means that we have never loved "all the way." We have never let it carry us through all its stages, all of its internal ecstasies, loneliness, and purifications. Maybe our very theological argument over grace and good works reveals our inability to put love and work together. To attain a whole and truly passionate sexuality is going to be hard work. We are going to have to want it more than almost anything else.

As the mystics always said, "God's love can be a thousand times harder than his justice." So can human love! And of this I am certain: it is God's love that we are afraid of, not God's justice. It is one another's goodness that we are protecting ourselves from, not the law.

God's way of loving is the only licensed teacher of human sexuality. God's passion created ours. Our deep desiring is a relentless returning to that place where all things are one. If we are afraid of our sexuality, we are afraid of God.

So once again, in Merton's fine phraseology, we must "make ready for the Christ, whose smile, like lightning, sets free the song of everlasting glory that now sleeps in your paper flesh."

AN APPETITE FOR WHOLENESS

In reflecting on human sexuality it is important that we distinguish between sexuality and genitality. Most people use the first word to apply to both and thus create a blanket and almost useless kind of language that serves only to perpetuate myths and non-communication.

By sexuality, we mean that essential and all-pervasive complementarity between persons, and in a certain sense, between all living things. Life is attracted to life. Beauty is attracted to both beauty and brokenness—which is a good description of all that lives.

Life is fragmented and finite and yet part of a larger and attractive whole. We long to be one with this wholeness. We seem to need to give ourselves to the other, or at least, we are fascinated or attracted by it. One need only observe people in an airport, or on the street, or reading gossip or romance magazines, or listen to much of human conversation to know that people are energized and excited by other people.

This is sexuality. It is our energy for life and for communication. Without it, we would settle for a cold and metallic kind of life; all would be trapped in each one's own inner world with no need to reach out, no desire to care. The power of bonding, linkage, and compassion would be gone from the earth. At its core, therefore, sexuality is a constant expression of the Spirit.

God seemingly had to take all sorts of risks in order that we would not miss the one thing necessary: we had to be called and even driven out of ourselves by an almost insatiable appetite so that we could never presume that we were self-sufficient. It is so important that we know that we are incomplete, needy, and essentially social that God had to create a life-force within us that would not be silenced — not until ten minutes after we are dead, they told us as novices! All this tells me that something very important is happening here, and it makes me glad that I am sexual — both attracting (I hope!) and endlessly attracted.

The very word comes from the Latin verb *secare*, meaning to cut or to divide. It reveals that primitive sense that something is separated here, and very likely longing to be reunited. But it is a reunion based on differentiation and complementarity. That is the power and energy of sexuality. It is the power of the opposite and the energy of a certain kind of opposition. Sexual attraction is a full continuum with the ultimate polarities being called masculine and feminine.

All of my experience as teacher, as counselor, as man, as a visitor to innumerable cultures, as well as my knowledge of history, tells me that men and women are obviously different. I agree that culture has taught all of us; and I do not have the skill to debate the eternal question between the influences of genes and environment. But if we are the same emotionally, psychically, or spiritually, one would think it would have shown itself in at least one age or culture. To be sure, we have trained and exaggerated some of the differences (usually to the advantage of the male), but let's hope that we will not lose the powerful complementary energy that is present in male-female sexuality for the sake of some doctrinaire philosophy of unisexuality.

It is our defined and affirmed identities as opposites that make for full creativity in sexuality. I suspect that is why God chose such an enacted encounter of opposition to be the focus for the continuation of all human, animal, and plant life. Sexuality is revealing something at the very heart of reality. It cherishes tension and builds on tension; but sexual union is always opposition overcome.

Genitality is a specific expression of our sexual selves. It does not cherish tension, but instead seeks release from tension. And that puts genitality in an entirely different situation. It cannot be treated the same as sexuality, but at the same time will never be understood unless we have first been accepted as and have grown as sexual men and women.

Genitality is that strictly biological and anatomical complementarity associated with the sexual organs and with the primary sexual characteristics. By definition we are dealing with a "part," but a part that is so hormonally and psychologically triggered that it is the literal preoccupation of much of the human race.

The genital, or the preoccupation with results, has kept many people from the much deeper process of communication and caring that gives us such profound joy. They have pandered to their exclusively genital, visual, or physical fascinations and find that they are almost incapable of full human relationship and affection. Simply put, human beings cannot be oriented toward their own pleasure and immediate gratification and communicate bonding love to another person at the same time.

Many people do not know simply how to enjoy or play or give pleasure to another. I cannot imagine what these people are going to do in heaven. It is not that God will exclude them from the communion of saints; it is just that many will be bored and unprepared for the leisure and playfulness of eternal love.

True and observed sexual encounter has much to teach us about spirituality. It is a school of growth and conversion, and not just the proverbial garden of forbidden delights. Maybe that is why a lot of people avoid full sexuality and remain just genital. Genitality is the ritual. Sexual intimacy is the reality.

We would be naive, however, if we denied that there is an almost mystical aura that surrounds the shapes and images of the human body. One need only observe the fertility rites, the phallic stones, the painted nudes since time immemorial. I am sure that we are dealing with images and archetypes so deeply rooted in the human psyche that we can never truly dismiss or deny them. Even religions and cultures, with all their warnings and taboos, only disguise and sometimes sublimate the power of these sexual images.

Perhaps our biggest shortcoming in the area of Christian sexual mores is that we have failed to realize that all love is dangerous. Love is very threatening to our existing worldview and our present ego boundaries. Yet love is better than any of the other alternatives. It is a risk that we must take to be human, and according to John "anyone who fails to love can never know God" (1 John 4:8).

The risk, fear, and discipline involved in loving rightly, I believe, cause people to use religion to avoid the tremendous amount of darkness and suffering that goes into the mature development of any human relationship. It is easier to simply quote the appropriate chapter and verse, or the cultural teaching, than to deal with the self and the potential beloved at my doorstep.

In all honesty, the Scripture scholar is surprised to find how little direct teaching Jesus gives us on sexual morality. It is obviously not his main concern: that is reserved for the proclamation of the kingdom of God and the call to forgiveness and reconciliation. This does not mean that sexual morality is unimportant, but that Jesus seems to feel that sexual practice will take care of itself if these primary teachings are deeply received.

They, too, are concerned with the creative overcoming of opposition.

I believe that there are two basic texts in the Gospels that teach us Jesus' positive understanding of "purity."

> The lamp of the body is the eye. It follows that if your eye is sound, your whole body will be filled with light. But if your eye is diseased, your whole body will be all darkness. If then, the light inside you is darkness, what darkness that will be. (Matthew 6:22-23)

Here Jesus tells us that it is all a matter of seeing. It is possible to have "light" inside of us that is not really light, answers that are not really wisdom. And Jesus comes not so much to fill our minds with the right answers as to open our minds so that we can see for ourselves.

The Christian virtue of purity is the ability to see as God sees. It is the long-suffering path toward seeing the truth, toward the vision of the whole. Impurity, therefore, is the partial vision. Impurity is to be satisfied with lies. It is to define ourselves as merely material and to limit ourselves to merely external observation.

Jesus here gives us responsibility for who we are and what we are becoming. We can educate our eyes to see what is really there, what is fully there. That will be a lamp, a light to illumine the "whole body."

The second basic text in Jesus' sexual teaching follows from the first:

> You have learnt how it was said: You must not commit adultery. But I say this to you: if a man looks at a woman lustfully, he has already committed adultery with her in his heart. If your right eye should cause you to sin, tear it out and throw it away; for it will do you less harm to lose one part of you than to have your whole body thrown into hell. And if your right hand should cause you to sin,

cut it off and throw it away, for it will do you less harm
to lose one part of you than to have your whole body go
to hell. (Matthew 5:27-30)

Again, we see Jesus' emphasis on the eye and the way that
we see one another. The real import of this passage from his
inaugural sermon is not that he is trying to teach us the immor-
ality of sexual thoughts and desires; he is telling us that we
should not try to separate what cannot be separated. We are a
history. We are one, we are whole, we are body, mind, spirit.
We are a truth. We are a story. We must put the chapters
together and read ourselves as a whole.

Purity is always wholistic. Impurity is invariably fragmented.
Goodness holds opposites together in the same place. Evil
always divides — and, in that, is conquered. Purity always integrates, putting eye, and heart, and body together. Impurity
separates and pretends that I am just body, or I am just this
moment or I am just need. And sometimes with equal igno-
rance, it pretends that I am just spirit.

Jesus says that if any part of yourself is keeping you from
being your full self, then you must cast off the false self at all
costs. All must be confessed and integrated.

"Every thought is our prisoner, captured to be brought into
obedience to Christ" (2 Corinthians 10:5). This does not mean
that we change the thoughts, or deny the thoughts, or disguise
the thoughts, or repress the thoughts. It means that we situate
them in the context of everything else. We refuse to believe
their lies. We refuse to idolize them or trust their overstated
promises.

But we do listen to them, their roots, their sources, their
many-colored motivations. We enjoy their life-energy, their
power for good, and we recognize their deception and power
for death. In that creative dialogue and tension, human passion
is born and warm affection is kindled. Such is the true and
profound sexuality that God is creating in us. Without such

tension, we have only momentary orgasm and passing flirtations.

When the seemingly bodily action recognizes that it is also mind, spirit, past and future, when it respects its physical self, without letting the body become a tyrant or dictator, then our sexual behavior is life-giving and obedient to the Maker. An action is evil or immoral when it is falsely centered and isolated from the rest of our lives. When an action is not integrated, then it is literally disintegrating of the person that God is creating. When we isolate parts of ourselves from one another, when we make use of our bodies for reasons other than the communication of truth, we are lessened and corrupted.

Without going into it at great length here, since it would make for an entire treatise on law and morality, we might just say that the traditional Christian ethic on sexual morality is in great part an accurate reflection of what is usually good and usually evil. It did not hang around this long merely through the efforts of moralistic clerics, but very likely because it represents the recurring experience of cultures and centuries as to what has created life and what has created death.

At the same time, the "law" is severely limited in its ability to lead us to all truth. That, as we know, is the work of the Spirit (John 16:13). Many have followed the law and never known love. Many have kept the law perfectly—and all for what? This most subtle link between Spirit and law is the crux of much of Jesus' teaching and the issue that brings Paul to such exhortation in both Romans and Galatians.

We have the wisdom and the experience in the Judeo-Christian tradition to fashion a positive morality, a morality that cuts a clean path between the rationalized libertinism of the modern age and the prudish guilt of the past. There is a way for the law to serve the Spirit. But there is absolutely no way that any guidelines will be workable apart from the Spirit of God working within us.

Moral sexuality might well be described as an "emotional sincerity" that shows itself in truthful relationships. It is a combination of sensitivity, responsibility, communication, constancy, and honesty in the ways that we share our lives and bodies with one another. We can tell truths with our bodies, and we can tell lies with them. Sexual relationships apart from personal responsibility for one another's larger lives is rightly called using another person.

The marriage promises must be held sacred if human words and intentions are to have any value. The indissolubility of this bond and promise must always remain the ideal and all-pervasive goal: "They are no longer two, but one body. What God has united, man must not divide" (Mark 10:9). Looks, thoughts, and desires must be subjected to this larger picture of truth. Otherwise they enslave us and make caring relationships impossible, trapping us in the vice of lust.

> Nothing the world has to offer: the sensual body, the lustful eye, the life of empty show, could ever come from the Father, but only from the world; and the world with all that it craves for is coming to an end, but anyone who does the will of God remains forever. (1 John 2:16-17)

As always the Word of God retains its truly idol-crashing character. First, it tells us that we are created in the image of God as male and female, and that this blessing allows us to be fruitful and to fill the earth (Genesis 1:27-28). Our sexual humanity is affirmed and identifies us with the very creativity of God.

But our sexuality remains gift only if we recognize its inherent tendency to domination and enslavement. Lust has a huge ego which demands total control and longs to take a central position that is reserved for the Lord himself. The "world" (John's word) and the "flesh" (Paul's word) are not bad in themselves, but only insofar as they blind and take over.

The biblical teaching on sexual morality is contingent on the larger reality which Jesus calls the kingdom of God. Unless one's life is given to the purposes and the seeking of this new and full reality, sexual morality becomes no more than a fear-ridden conglomeration of social taboos — with God to back them up.

The virtue of sexual purity is one effect of a mature life in the Spirit. Impurity cannot be forced or legislated out of our minds and hearts, it simply becomes superfluous and unnecessary as we become more whole. It falls away like an unsightly cocoon, as we gradually learn what matters, what lasts, and what is real. Impurity finally shows itself for the illusion that it is.

My desire and fond intention in these reflections has been to initiate a healthy and holy dialogue within your own spirit and perhaps between would-be lovers. In such an interchange, I hope that you will catch sight of that one Holy Spirit, who is enlivening us all and assuring us that it is from our flesh that we shall look on God (Job 19:26).

MARRIAGE AND CELIBACY

"I have married a wife, and therefore I cannot come" (Luke 14:18-20). Surely this has to be the strangest of all responses to Christ's beckoning. How could anyone imagine that marital love would conflict with "the love that moves the sun and moon and the other stars"?

And yet Jesus implies that if the two calls are honestly in conflict there is no doubt about the absolute primacy of the call to the kingdom. Before one can enthrone faithful married love, he or she first has to dethrone it in favor of God's love. One's journey toward understanding leads to a right ordering of love, so that married love can be insured, nurtured, and protected.

This ordering of love in terms of the kingdom frees Jesus further from the world's agenda so that he can even recommend and himself live the unthinkable: "There are some who are celibate for the sake of the kingdom. Let anyone accept this who can" (Matthew 19:12). Later we see that Paul seemed to live and understand this same call (1 Corinthians 7:7, 25). As he advises others, so he himself seems to "have firmly made his mind up, without any compulsion and in complete freedom of choice" (7:37). A new and free and open space is being created by the love between the Father and the Son.

Absolute newness, *creatio ex nihilo* (creating from nothing), is always an assurance that the Spirit has been heard. Free celibacy, impossible for the world, is therefore a most radical sign of the kingdom. But if celibacy has come upon hard times even within the bosom of the church, it is likely because the church has lost its sense of intimacy and familial relatedness, which support the charism of true celibacy.

We are seeing the gift arise quite naturally among some of our most healthy and receptive members in community. It is not tied to any sense of ministry, efficiency, or "victim offering," but appears to be a deep word of truth that is heard in the context of personal prayer and real sharing. It is a sense of vocation and integrity which, like all prophetic actions, has a hard time explaining itself or justifying itself to anyone else — and often even to the individual who has chosen it. It is an absolute newness, which says that God is sufficient, but it is also an absolute solitude, which says the world is lonely and passing away.

Celibacy is communion with the ever-new God and compassion for the old and tired world. As communities open to the whole tradition evolve, the charism of celibacy is sure to blossom with new freshness and creativity.

The accepted order of family relationships and sexual roles in American culture is not encouraging us to uncover the freedom that the gospel offers us. It seems that we might have to create communities where this growth is really expected of us or even demanded of us before we are going to learn more constructive patterns of human relationship.

Our age tends to be much more in touch with its shadow than with itself. If we are to believe the testimony of much, if not most, of modern drama, literature, and cinema, we are, in fact, almost obsessed with our shadow. Modern humanity is so aware of its darkness (while refusing to call it darkness!) that it seems to doubt that there is anything beyond the shadow. Humanity is therefore largely controlled by the shadow and imprisoned within half of its soul. Church tradition would call this original sin.

It is not surprising that the tradition would also say that the only antidote to original sin is baptism, which is the initiation rite into the Christian community. We still have baptism. But what, practically, is it initiating people into?

We do not have many functional Christian communities which can walk the journey with us and help us discern between darkness and light, our shadow and our true selves in Christ. We need relationships of duration and truth "to unveil our faces so that we can reflect like mirrors the brightness of the Lord." In Christian community we will "all grow brighter and brighter as we are gradually turned into the image that we reflect; this is the work of the Lord who is Spirit" (2 Corinthians 3:18).

We know ourselves only in mirrors, only in relationship. God's life is always mediated. We wait in darkness, unaware of ourselves, living in illusions and shadows, as C. S. Lewis says, "until we have faces." There is such a fear of our unknown selves and a concomitant fear of our sexuality that people in general are unable to trust or entrust themselves to other people.

Our sexuality is our symbolic self. It cannot be treated lightly and must be allowed to come to consciousness. There must be a safe and trusting place where this can be allowed to happen, or our symbolic self will remain in the world of guilt, repression, and unconsciousness, where it will indirectly but certainly control us.

One of the most hopeful signs in familial church communities is that these issues have a safe environment where they can be dealt with openly. It is OK to show affection here, and it does not mean that we are leading up to a genital relationship. It is acceptable to *feel* here, and you do not have to be afraid or ashamed. Of course, you are going to fall in love! That is the meaning of life. I hope it happens many, many times.

In community it can happen creatively, "in spirit and in truth," but not without great pain. I am convinced that the problem with so much aberrant sexuality today is not that people feel too much desire or too much passion, but rather that they do not feel enough. We must find a place where we can feel the full range and greatness of human emotion, the agony and the ecstasy, and therefore put our sexuality in healthy perspective.

For Jesus, the kingdom is the possibility of universal compassion: it is community and not just kindly coupling. Marriage is a school, a sacrament and a promise of the coming kingdom, but not itself the final stage. Jesus dethrones married love in order to enthrone it in proper perspective. The specific love points to the universal, but only the "love that moves the sun, the moon, and the other stars" can finally protect and preserve and make possible the specific love of a man and a woman.

Jesus seems to be concerned about widening the family circle to include all the life that God is offering. He knows how paralyzing and even deadening the familial relationships can be when they have cut their lifelines from the larger truth and more universal love. Family can be both life and death. Church also can be both life and death. Church and blood family both have the greatest power to wound and the greatest power to heal.

The gospel believes in family, but it is never going to limit itself to the blood relationships and call that alone family: "Anyone who prefers father or mother to me is not worthy of me. Anyone who prefers son or daughter to me is not worthy of me." Good American Christian religion would never dare to say those words on its own. When we do, we recite them falteringly, because we cannot really understand the radical nature of Jesus' vision.

Paul develops Jesus' teaching in the context of his faith communities. He is convinced of the supreme importance of shared faith and shared life within the marriage partnership: "Do not refuse each other except by mutual consent, and then only for an agreed time, to devote yourselves to prayer" (1 Corinthians 7:5). With our unintegrated emphasis on sexual relationship today, it would be hard to imagine the Christian leader who would have the courage to preach on that text today without feeling naive or old-fashioned. The absolute primacy of the kingdom is no longer agreed upon among believers. Prayer is not conceived as a possible stronger bonding than intercourse.

If the community model of church has seldom taken hold, it can probably be attributed to many causes: individualism, authoritarianism, clericalism, fear, plus an overly intellectualized communication of the gospel. But the cause that I would like to deal with here is a certain kind of apathy (*a pathos*: no feeling), a fear of passion, which has consistently and ironically kept our incarnational faith from dealing with relationships, sexuality, emotions, bodiliness, and the power of love in general.

I am hard put to find a single century in our 2,000-year history since the Word became flesh in which there has been consistent and positive church teaching on the sexuality of this enfleshed creation. We have run from it, denied it, camouflaged it, sublimated it, died to it, sacramentalized it (thank God!) — but we have only in rare and mature instances really faced it, integrated it, and allowed it to raise us to God. We are afraid of the Word become flesh, we are afraid of heaven much more than we are afraid of hell. We live in an endless fear of the passion of God, who feels fiercely.

I believe that for this more than any other reason the church has historically avoided seeing itself as family and as community. To do so would have necessitated relationships. It would have involved feeling, especially love and anger, and intolerable passion. It would have necessitated communion and communication instead of law and dogma. It would have necessitated a Christian way of life instead of efficient and impersonal religious service stations. It would necessitate really wrestling with the angel of Yahweh instead of just reading about him, proving him, and using him to legitimate our cultural biases.

Quite frankly, it would necessitate falling in love and losing a bit of precious control. It would lead us into pursuit of understanding when what we want is certainty.

Maybe it could all be characterized as a crisis of friendship. Is caring and compassion capable of being structured into a society? Can we expect it and factor it into the process, or will it always be a gift, a surprise, a bit of an enigma in a world of structured conflict?

We have so accepted the functional and the competitive nature of most human relationships that any deep friendship between two men or two women is immediately suspect of homosexuality. We are all affected by this climate of fear and mistrust of ourselves and of others. The usual solution is to remain aloof, since there is no support system which can hold on to us through the ups and downs of darkness and light.

The natural family has shown itself incapable of meeting the crisis. The spiritual family of the church has the right theory, but lacks the practice, experience, and lifestyle setting. We need quite simply to found places of sharing where the Word can be shared, and where hearts and bread can be broken and passed around.

John Henry Newman said that "so much holiness is lost to the church because brothers refuse to share the secrets of their hearts one with another." This intellectual giant had as his cardinal's motto, *Cor ad cor loquitur*, "Heart speaks to heart."

If the church is to be renewed, if family is to happen anywhere, we must again make it possible for heart to speak to heart. All else will finally show itself to be doctrinaire and ideological, but heart speaking to heart, little places of sharing the truth, have every chance of being the "two or three gathered in His name." These will be the places of incarnation from which Christ will again be born.

COMMUNITY

God's Strategy for the Reluctant Church

BUILDING FAMILY

The real way to be biblical and to respect biblical authority is to do what biblical people did, and in the way that they did it. It is not to quote biblical sources or uncover the deep and secret meanings of biblical texts. The authority of words, even inspired words, must somehow be based in the *de facto* authority of accomplished deeds, redeemed peoples, and living bodies. In other words, it has to have worked somewhere, sometime, with someone, or it is an idealized abstraction. I find that a great many people who put themselves under the cope of religion are, in fact, people who enjoy ideology and abstraction as an escape from real commitment and real conversion.

A salvation history is the beginning and the basis of Christian and Jewish theology. Historical events gave authority to the words and allowed them to be written down with inspiration. Moses did not give endless teachings about Abrahamic faith; he led people out of slavery, through a desert, and into a whole new place. He created a new people who could begin to hear God.

47

The prophets did not give weekly sermons on Moses and timely tips from Leviticus; they read the signs of the times, saw God acting, deposed kings, and shook nations. The prophets purified the people that Moses had created when they had grown tired of paying the price of peoplehood.

Jesus himself did not find his authority in words or traditions; he taught with living authority "and not like the scribes" (Mark 1:22). With the apostles and disciples he again created a new people, a spiritual family. And he did this most simply and profoundly by telling this family about their Father and the full nature of his love.

This had the frightening effect of establishing totally new love bonds and re-aligning family relationships into what we would eventually call "church." " 'And who are my mother and my brothers?' And looking around at those sitting in a circle about him, he said, 'Here are my mother and my brothers. Anyone who does the will of my Father, that person is my brother and sister and mother' " (Mark 3:34).

I don't think we have begun to plumb the depths of Jesus' radical response. Only those who had first heard the Baptist's call to fill valleys and level mountains (Luke 3:5) would be ready for Jesus. The rest of us continue to avoid forming God's new family in favor of some form of spiritualism, legalism, biblicism, or rationalism.

But God creates around each of his chosen ones a network of committed relationships. In these faithful and suffering relationships, God can be rightly known. Outside of them, God and his good news are continually used, abused, and distorted. He remains word, instead of Word-become-flesh. He is argued about instead of loved. He is proven instead of shared. He is religion instead of life.

God is telling us that he takes human life seriously. What we have to do to come into this world—discover ourselves as either son, daughter, brother, sisters, mother, or father—is not just a time-consuming preliminary. It is, in fact, the whole of the process. The end is summed up in the beginning.

Baptism, our initiation into the new family of God, is everything-all-at-once, symbolized and celebrated. It takes the rest of our life to understand it, to suffer it, and to appropriate it. The reality precedes the word, and gives authority to the word. The reality must be lived first and only then spoken about. The Christian life is a matter of becoming who we already are.

The reality is Trinity; God is shared life, life in relationship. Church is the communion of saints; family is both the beginning and the end. Only in that context can Bible and sacraments be fittingly interpreted and understood.

In the experience of the natural and spiritual family the word becomes teachable, powerful, and enduring enough to be written down with authority. In any other context, it becomes another head trip: "So you, my friends, have died to the law by becoming identified with the body of Christ, and accordingly you have found another husband in him ... but we are discharged from the law, to serve God in a new way, the way of the Spirit, in contrast to the old way, the way of a written word" (Romans 7:4, 6).

I say this not to discredit the scriptures. They are spirit and life for me. But we must find the true basis for a working scriptural authority, which is now all but lost to our critical world. Our formula during the last individualistic centuries has been something like this:

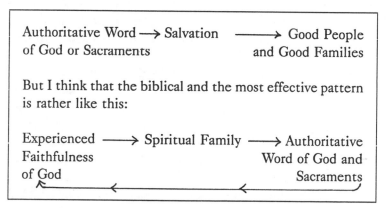

Authoritative Word ⟶ Salvation ⟶ Good People
of God or Sacraments   and Good Families

But I think that the biblical and the most effective pattern is rather like this:

Experienced ⟶ Spiritual Family ⟶ Authoritative
Faithfulness   Word of God and
of God   Sacraments

God's basic building block for self-communication is not the "saved" individual, or the rightly informed believer, or even personal careers in ministry, but precisely the journey and bonding process that God initiates in marriages, families, tribes, nations, peoples, and churches who are seeking to involve themselves in his love.

The body of Christ, the spiritual family, is God's strategy. It is both medium and message. It is both beginning and end: "May they all be one . . . so that the world may believe it was you who sent me . . . that they may be one as we are one, with me in them and you in me" (John 17:21, 23).

There is no other form for the Christian life except a common one. This may even be a matter of culture, if culture refers to something which is shared and passed on. In this sense, I am wondering if there is any other kind of Christianity except "cultural Christianity."

Until and unless Christ is someone happening between people, the gospel remains largely an abstraction. Until he is passed on personally through faithfulness and forgiveness, through bonds of union, I doubt whether he is passed on at all.

We are now paying the price for centuries in which the Church was narrowed from a full vision of peoplehood to an almost total preoccupation with private persons and their devotional needs. But history has shown that individuals who are confirmed in their individualism by the very character of our evangelism will never create church, except after the model of a service station: they will use it as a commodity like everything else.

Certainly, we must deal with individuals. But I find that these many churched individuals often do not even know what the questions of the gospel life are. As a result, we find ourselves using most of our personnel and institutions to give fairly good answers to completely inappropriate questions that have nothing to do with community life. We are saving souls while God is creating a people.

The very nature of our lifestyle and our church teaching

must say from the beginning what the goal is — the communion of saints, a shared life together as family, the trinitarian life of God, the kingdom. Then we must deal with individuals in the church as they are on the journey toward that goal.

I am absolutely convinced that it is out of this context, and the set of felt needs which arise from it, that the New Testament is written for our instruction. If we are not asking the appropriate questions — and I dare to say it — the Bible will do us and those around us more harm than good. It will be a power in the hands of those who do not know what to do with that much power. Thus the sad history of Western Christianity!

The prophet Haggai criticizes the Jews after the exile for individually hurrying to repanel the walls of their own houses, while the common walls of the temple lie in ruins (Haggai 1:4, 9). His prophetic call is now and forever. We still think that we can work with the world's agenda, where career and individual fulfillment are the basic building blocks of society. And we believe that we can build church from those well-educated and well-saved blocks. But God needs "living stones making a spiritual house" (1 Peter 2:5).

For Jesus, such teachings as forgiveness, healing, and justice are not just a spiritual test course. They are quite simply the necessary requirements for a basic shared life. Peacemaking and reconciliation are not some kind of box seat tickets to heaven. They are the price of peoplehood. They express the truth in the heart of God, the truth that has been shared with us in the Holy Spirit, the union in Jesus who is reconciling all people to himself.

A trinitarian God is a God in relationship. He both knows and is known. He loves and is loved. He believes and is believed in. We come to know who he is through the very same dialogue.

We come to be in this world through a relationship called marriage and family. We come into the kingdom through a set of relationships called church or spiritual family. The same rules for the creation of life, the sharing of life, and the destruction of life apply in both the natural family and the spiritual family, and therefore, in our very relationship with God. It all becomes very real and very simple. The areas in our life where we cannot be shared are the very areas where God cannot touch us. And the areas that we cannot let God touch will never be shared for the good of all.

The natural family and the spiritual family seem to need one another for correct image, focus, and direction. The natural family without the spiritual family becomes isolated, insulated, inbred, and without vision. The spiritual family without the natural family has become cold, ideological, impersonal, task-oriented, and unable to carry out its purposes. All in-depth renewal is somehow a return to family.

My experience is that powerful spiritual growth usually happens in the context of the healing, restoring, and recreating of the original familial relationships. Both Elijah and John the Baptist are seen to have the role of "turning the hearts of fathers toward their children and the hearts of children toward their fathers" (Malachi 3:24, Luke 1:17). Without their precursory work, Jesus cannot do his work.

What the natural family should intuitively know, the spiritual family teaches through the graced dynamic of sin, conversion, and redemption. The spiritual family enables us to reform, renew, and relive the natural family and its relationships. The very practical and mundane needs of the natural family should keep the church from pie-in-the-sky theologizing. It should keep us concerned about a very real and ennobling salvation, about justice, peace, lifestyle, unity, and healing—the kind of things Jesus concerned himself with in his ministry.

We are saddled and bridled today with a religion that is not sure if it wants to become church. Its adherents' expectations are very set. It is a comfortable and very materialistic religion, which tests its people's commitment on the level of doctrine but is afraid to test that commitment on issues of lifestyle or mature conscience.

We give out bits of advice on marriage and family life, while the very structure of family crumbles all around us. Could it be that our vocation is not to teach about family, but to ourselves *become* family and to submit to its disciplines? If the world no longer knows how to struggle for unity and maintain commitments at the cost of pain, could it be because the church, the sign of salvation, has not traveled the narrow road first? In a commodity world we have become a commodity church. We have allowed the gospel to become something we buy and sell to others, something we use for power and good feeling. We have done to God what we do quite comfortably to one another—we use him!

But family cannot ever be used. It can only be created, waited for, enjoyed, and lost. Family is the last holdout of the non-utilitarian mode. It will not allow you to make it into a commodity. It must teach the church its living world so that the church can teach the world how life is generated, how faith is shared, and how God is love.

The best teachers of Christ are without doubt fathers and mothers, sons and daughters, brothers and sisters. For in their embrace, faith is not really taught at all. It is caught, almost by accident, as they struggle to remain in union one with another.

"I am writing this because I want you to know how to behave in God's family—that is, the church of the living God, which upholds the truth and keeps it safe" (1 Timothy 3:14-15).

CHARTING COMMUNITY GROWTH

Communities are living organisms. Communities are marriages. Communities are relationships. They grow through somewhat predictable stages. The style, color, timing, and energy of these stages will differ according to a thousand and one different factors that cannot be controlled. It is often difficult to discern any constant patterns. However, there are some universal shifts and crises that any living body must go through in order to grow up.

I am mostly referring to communities held together by trust.

Other types of communities might be held together by law, proximity, function, economic advantage, or specific goal orientation. But those communities whose primary motivation is faith have come together because they trust that God is doing something, that God is calling them to participate in what is happening; and as a result, they want to grow in trusting one another as they together trust the Lord.

This is undoubtedly the most difficult type of community in which to live. It is by far the most powerful. Every stage is a release of energy that can be either negative or positive, or maybe even both. Wisdom is in touch with this power. It is able to recognize and discern which energy is unto life and which is unto death: "But these are the very things that God has revealed to us through the Spirit, for the Spirit reaches the depths of everything, even the depths of God" (1 Corinthians 2:10).

We have become convinced in our nine years of community building at New Jerusalem that you can only build on life. All else is sand. You cannot build on fear, guilt, coercion, or even idealism. You cannot build on gospel passages, church commandments, or papal mandates, unless they are finally putting you in touch with life.

You cannot build on death. Unforgiveness, repressed hurts, denied feelings, unconscious anger will all eventually show themselves as unfit foundations for community. They might appear to be energy in the short run, but they will in time show themselves to be negative energy, incapable of real life. "Wisdom builds herself a house" (Proverbs 9:1). And wisdom knows that you can only build on the foundation of life.

This journey into ever deeper life is the essence of faith community. It demands at least a few people who have made the journey on some level before. Some, or maybe just one, have to have developed an eye for life and death. They will recognize some of the pitfalls, temptations, and traps along the way.

No matter what their official role or function or title, these people will be the leaders of the community. They will have the power, because they are in touch with the sources of power and the drain-offs of power. It is not even necessary that these people hold the formal power in the community, as long as they are in healthy dialogue with those who do. The life can be transferred, and the body will grow.

There are four stages of community which use this wisdom about life and death.

Stage One

In order to have a good middle and a good end, you must have a good beginning. Just because it is Stage One does not mean that it is unimportant and can be quickly jumped over in order to get into the "real thing." Fortunately or unfortunately, we do not usually know that we are in Stage One. We are probably not aware that community is about to happen. We are uniquely in the power of the Spirit. It is usually unprogrammed, unplanned, and unsuspected. It is usually pure gift. Only years later do we become aware of the power available and given at the beginning.

This phenomenon is probably what people are referring to when they speak of things "beginning charismatically and ending institutionally." Perhaps this is the only way that it can really happen, and why we constantly need new beginnings, breaks with the past, or at least a return to the power that is inherent in the mythic first stage.

We cannot maintain the fervor and euphoria of Stage One for very long. If we try—as many groups do—we will pay a very high price: We will have to choose blindness. It is a great and very subtle temptation precisely because stage one appears to be so holy, inspired, and empowered. It is not unlike the first blush of romantic love, and no one wants to let go of it.

Stage One is a type of passive dependency. We have not necessarily discovered a new life within ourselves, but we have instead discovered it in another, in the group, in the vision. We lean on them heavily, because we are drawing life from them and they are putting us in touch with the depths of our own dreaming. It is very nearly the only way that we can begin, even though it is a kind of blind listening. It is not a deep listening to the self, but an enthrallment in what is "out there" or what we have together. But ironically it is not really a love of these things. It is still a clear, but absolutely necessary, love of the self. We are in love with what the dream does for us, what the community brings out of us, what others give to us.

Lest we snobbishly pull up our nose at such puerile and disguised motivation, let me be quick to say that at least it is trust. At least it reveals a capacity for wonder, and awe, and desire. It is dependency on another, recognition of life within another, and therefore the beginnings of love. Pity the poor folk who are not capable of Stage One. And many today are not—because they refuse to release their hearts to any group or individual who is not formed and perfect and worthy of their self-donation.

The consistent experience of history is that love and communities and, in fact, most events that enlist the commitment of people have largely non-rational beginnings. If we are waiting around for something to appear in which we can invest ourselves from a position of total, objective detachment, then we want a job perhaps, but we do not want a community. Certainly we do not want a community of faith.

Faith is very likely the most free and most fully personal response that a human being can make. It includes intellect, will, and affection. But it is only the beginning. The Lord, it seems, is out to integrate us—not just excite us.

Stage Two

Here is where the trouble begins. We would rather remain blind than see what we begin to see in Stage Two: The community is imperfect. And so is the leader, the vision, the structure, the timing, the theology, the initial call, the present situation, and the tuna casserole that was served for lunch. The patterns of Stage Two are as many as the leaves on the trees, but that it will come is absolutely certain. It must come if love and light are ever to happen.

This is the desert, the wilderness, the dark night of the soul, the time of temptation. Many leave, get divorced or discouraged during this time. There is a loss of perspective and a loss of nerve. Many rational types of problems will appear, but this is basically an emotional journey that must be walked through with both the emotions and the head together. It is a letting-go of control, and this is what we do not want to do. We begin to experience our inadequacy and our need and know deeply and darkly that we are imperfect, that we are sinners. And then we have to be converted in order to live.

Stage Two is a period of non-listening to others, to the Lord, and even to ourselves. It is a state of alienation and discouragement, in which we should never make major decisions or too quickly trust our first emotional responses. Our emotions are being stretched; they are growing. They will embarrass us, frighten us, and serve our relationships rather poorly during this time. But the greatest mistake would be either to deny them or believe them totally in order to reassert control. We must, however, be free to *feel* them, both the negative and the positive.

And blessed are we if we have a true and wise friend to walk with us during this darkness. We need someone who will not just correct us or just caress us, but who can say, "I have been here before." We need the sister or brother who can assure us that there is light in this period and not just darkness. Most difficult of all, we need to have given them enough authority beforehand so that we will believe what they say when nothing else within us wants to believe it.

It is in Stage Two that we have the greatest lack of wisdom and understanding. Most church communities have foolishly chosen to remain in Stage One rather than venture into this great and terrible wilderness. Individuals have often been forced to go it alone. This destroyed many, and made saints out of some. But the desert was God's chosen journey to make saints out of *all* the people.

Competent spiritual direction is perhaps the only way through. Yet it is one of the most noticeably absent gifts in many attempts at community today. For too long we held our communities together by law, fear, tradition, and social pressure. Now that we are trying to form truly voluntary and healing communities, we find that we need spiritual directors more than "heads"; we need real spiritual authority instead of just "superiors." We need people who understand darkness, and by their presence can hold us through to the light.

Stage Three

Turn around! Believe the good news! The breakthrough to Stage Three is a moment of grace that exceeds even the amazing grace that breaks us into Stage One.

Only now does love really begin. We still know everything that we knew in Stage Two. We know that we live in an imperfect world and with an imperfect self; but we are freed to love anyway. Here we can begin to speak of adult Christianity, because now we have the beginnings of free persons who are capable of decision and response, and therefore of faith.

In the first two stages, we are largely dealing with reaction, experiment, and divine initiative. Now life is beginning to recognize life. We are choosing—not out of fear or need or convenience—to respond to a call. Grace has met its mark.

We are now looking back at God with the very eyes with which God once looked at us. And yet they are now *our* eyes. That is the one and only miracle after the incarnation.

Stage-Three people are the creators of community. Their very freedom draws life around them. They seem to draw their life from within themselves and are, in this sense, healthily independent. They do not really need community, it appears. And yet they decide for what God has decided for. They choose to participate, to share in the pain and life of God for the sake of God's kingdom. They know that they do not *have* to do this, and yet they *must* do it to be who they already are.

Stage-Three people are not passively dependent; they are positively dependent. They face the need of being human. They choose to need, just as the Father needs the Son and the Son needs the Father. They agree to the trinitarian life within.

Shared life is the only life possible because God is shared life. Community is no longer a way of life. Community *is* life. And God is perfect community.

You must have at least one — hopefully several — Stage-Three people in order to form a community. Sometimes, like Moses and Miriam, they are themselves formed on the same journey that they are leading. These are the sisters and brothers who can say to us floundering around in Stages One and Two, "I have been here before. Come, let's walk together."

A community where many or even the majority of the members have at least once broken through to Stage Three is a delightful and holy place to live. It is a true foretaste of the coming kingdom and the communion of saints. Here real virtue and heroism are possible. Here honest communication begins. True listening and healthy obedience are no threat.

We can at last deal with real issues and not just projections, fears, and reactions. Words become truly helpful and even beautiful because they come from deep and quiet places within. The community is no longer used to simply work out personal goals and agendas, but it is seen and enjoyed as an end in itself. Community now has the possibility of becoming family. And yet there is more.

Stage Four

There is another moment of response that must be spoken of. It is surely the triumph of grace. It is the goal toward which we move and for which all good pastors work as they teach their communities. It is the stage of perfect listening, perfect responsiveness, perfect love. Stage Four is the stuff that saints are made of. Stage Four is what the world is longing to see in our Christianity. The wise world always believes Stage Four and easily recognizes counterfeits. The irony is that people and communities can often fool themselves, even though the world will see through their disguise. Stage-One people often think that they are in Stage Four. They are out of touch with the whole, and interpret their exciting part as if it were a perfect whole.

This deception has been so common in the history of religious movements and groups that people are understandably suspicious and mistrustful of idealistic people with pious platitudes and pretentions. They are right when they say, "Wait, and see." Saints do not happen overnight or at the age of twenty-one. Communities are not measured in years, but in decades or even centuries.

I speak of this deception because of the American phenomenon of religion, which includes so many Stage-Four pretensions in the guise of fundamentalist, charismatic, or even social-activist communities. As we have seen in the recent Moral Majority drama, such groups can gain influence far beyond their deserving, because the masses have no clear criteria for spiritual discernment.

Stage-Four communities come not to do their own will, but the will of the One who sends them. They are the clearest incarnation of Jesus in space and time. They do only what they hear God saying. They are known for what God is known for. They are free to succeed and free to fail. They are not just positively dependent on one another, but now they are interdependent and together facing the larger world. By their time and trials together they have discovered a basis for unity deeper than momentary differences. God goes on working, and so do they.

Such communities are ready for vocation and mission in the fullest sense. Some are very likely being raised up to face the faith problems of the next decades. Their intellects, their wills, and their emotions are even now being tried and tested to stretch to full capacity our desire and longing for unity.

Every attempt at faith community is a necessary participation in the eternal longing of God that we might be one. We would otherwise find little reason to hold out and hold on through these stages or any other stages of growth.

Growth does not just happen without the proper conditions. Two of those proper and necessary conditions are time and wisdom.

We probably go through these stages many different times in our life and in many different ways. But once we have experienced and chosen at least a Stage-Three existence, I doubt that we could ever again be satisfied with an ongoing Stage One or Two response. We would see it for what it is and again move on. Not to do so would probably be the real meaning of sin.

Hopefully, this growth journey will give us some helpful perspectives on what the Lord seems to be doing in many of our lives. Perhaps this has taught a few people who will themselves teach a few people about the one thing that is more precious than our life—and that is our life together.

AUTHORS OF LIFE TOGETHER

If you want to feel the aroma of Christianity, you must copy the rose. The rose irresistibly draws people to itself, and the scent remains with them. Even so, the aroma of Christianity is imparted in an even quieter and more imperceptible manner, if possible.

Mahatma Gandhi

Christianity has been largely filtered to the world through the mind and experience of Western civilization. Naturally, it has taken on many of that civilization's colorings and questions. It shows a preference for the words of Scripture which are supposedly active, rational, aggressive, decisive, conclusive, divisive, measurable, and provable. It usually neglects or at least fails to comprehend many other biblical teachings. As a result, much of Western Christianity lacks a deep inner authority and is forever caught up in disguised struggles to find that authority. More often than not, it settles for an extrinsic authority instead of the deep inner authority which alone can be called biblical faith.

Inner authority seems to come from "experiencing our experiences," and experiencing them as deeply our own. Most people seem to be satisfied with gathering their authority in the form of ideas, opinions, and quotes from significant sources. They might control their information in rather creative ways, but it is obvious that the authority is outside themselves. They might even have an authoritative role or function, but they are not themselves sources of power, energy, or life.

We seem intuitively to be able to recognize the difference. We might *need* to be close to the authoritative role; but we will usually *want* to be close to the authoritative person. They "author" us. They create life in us. They seem to write life more than they are written upon. As with Jesus, power comes out from them.

This does not mean that people with inner authority are rare and heroic. Their power need not be immediately noticeable or highly charismatic. It is commonly much more shaded and subtle.

Gandhi's rose gives us an appropriate image. The quiet and imperceptible authority of the rose comes from the fact that it is in fact beautiful, that it gives off a lovely fragrance. It does not need to prove itself or convert you to its side. It knows it is a rose. If you are a human being with a nose and an eye for beauty, you will recognize the inherent authority of the rose. In fact, its inner authority might well be so pressing and demanding that you might say to the rose, as did Francis de Sales, "Stop shouting!"

If Christianity relied on its inner authority, the weight of its truth and the sheer power of genuine goodness, the world would also say to Christians, "I hear you; stop shouting." And we would not have preached a sermon or spoken a single word.

When the world meets people whose center of gravity is within themselves and not just in religion or answers, the world will draw close like moths to a flame. When we meet people who know that they know, and know that they know so much more than they can understand, and finally have the trust and patience to remain in that knowledge, then we will have people who can truly represent the authority of God. In their presence we will grow strong.

There is usually a direct correlation between one's need and reliance upon mere external authority and one's lack of true inner authority. The communities of the future will no longer be able to survive, or make any lasting contribution, unless they are fostering and protecting a true inner authority in their members. Our communities will only be as strong as our individual members are strong.

Our age has become too sophisticated not to see through the old-time motives of fear, law, and "Scripture says so." It believes that the law is written on our hearts, and knows that Scripture will also be confirmed by the inner testimony of the Holy Spirit.

The authority that we need must be total. It can no longer come from mere church mandate or Bible interpretation, but it must also come from our souls. We need Christians who have souls!

The Catholic and Orthodox traditions have tended to substitute church authority for soul authority; the Protestant tradition has replaced soul with the Bible or individualism. Both sets of traditions are searching for the true seat and center of authority; that is precisely what religion purports to do.

But they are both at least one step removed from true authority. They have settled for the common religious substitute: law instead of spirit. They foster conformity instead of true biblical obedience, traditions instead of truthfulness, and mediocrity instead of faith. "The law killeth, but the Spirit alone gives life."

External authority is quickly grabbed onto precisely because people do not know, have not listened, studied, struggled, or prayed. In the realm of the Spirit, this is false coin. It is counterfeit. It is much easier to produce than the real thing.

But when the majority of people are using counterfeit coins, people forget what the real thing looks like. They, in fact, judge the real thing to be showy, unnecessary, or presumptuous. In the world of religion, inner authority is unfortunately considered threatening, divisive, and even fanatical. Those who operate from a free place within, not merely reacting to trends and traditions, are often thought to be overly conscientious or "taking themselves too seriously."

Dorothy Day, founder of the Catholic Worker movement, was fairly well ignored by both church and state in her lifetime. Only in death, when she cannot embarrass us anymore by the challenge of her life, do we admire and admit to her immense inner authority. She had soul. We all knew it, but were afraid to allow her to influence us too much. We had to protect ourselves from the rose by not looking.

We might say that we all knew it because she knew it first herself. People with inner authority recognize their center as within themselves. They draw life from this deep well. They are called self-starters by educators, labeled self-actualized in the schools of psychology, and named saints by the church. The canonization process is, of course, held up until long after death—one reason, perhaps, why Dorothy Day told those who would call her a saint, "Don't write me off that easily."

Those with inner authority draw life from within because there *is* a life within—not just laws, principles, duties, or fears, but life. And they know what wisdom has taught them: You can only build on life.

Ordinarily they do not attribute this life to themselves. They are insistent that the life is gift. They are anxious to give it away and call others into it since they know it cannot be earned, diminished, or hoarded. It is not theirs. They do not possess it as much as it possesses them.

Inner authority has no need to shore itself up or protect itself by status symbols. Jesus did not need to prove to anyone that he was the Son of God.

Inner authority lets truth speak for itself, allows other ideas to live or die on their own merits, and like love itself, "takes no pleasure in other peoples' sins but delights in the truth; it is always ready to excuse, to trust, to hope, and to endure whatever comes" (1 Corinthians 12:6-7). Only people with inner authority, what Gandhi called "soul force," are capable of true nonviolence. Only they can both let things be and call them into being. They alone create. All the rest of us simply rearrange.

Although many in a community may possess inner authority, certainly all true leaders do. That is why people follow and trust their leadership. That is also why people often have an ambivalent relationship with their leaders. They are at once in love with them, envious of them, and sometimes hate them for possessing what they want and fear they themselves do not have.

Leaders are the object of much community transference and projection. The most fundamental relationship in any group is between the group and its leader or leaders. The leader is the symbol of the deepest level of life within the group. He or she is the non-rational symbol of the group's power, but also of the group's weakness and fear of death. The members transfer to the leader their own fears and lack of inner authority.

The goal of good leadership is to promote the growth of inner authority among members. As they grow in their own inner authority, they will alternately love and hate those whom they once needed. They will have to find ever new reasons for trust and obedience. This is the necessary rhythm of growth. It probably explains many of the conflicts in community and also much of the burnout of leaders, who do not usually understand the emotional complexity of their role.

Human beings both worship and fear power. We are fascinated by those who have power in any form. We admire them, give them our loyalty, and depend on them because they put us in touch with our own inner power or desire for it. We find strength. But we usually do not know that this is happening.

When we do, we become ashamed and deny our need for the leader.

It is at this point that we desperately need clarity and wisdom. A kind of pride, what the Greeks called *hubris*, usually takes over and keeps us from a deeper truth.

In the classic Greek tragedies, the illusion of independence from the gods kept the hero from becoming a hero and himself becoming a god. We are afraid to admit that we are not essentially self-created (and neither is the leader), but all tied together in a chain of being and dependency whereby we all enter into deeper life.

We only come into inner authority insofar as we admit a positive and mature dependency on others and freely enter into a mature exchange of life and power. This is necessary and good. In fact, the Christian tradition has named it the communion of saints, the body of Christ.

Unfortunately, we are often resentful and mistrustful toward the very persons who might do for us what we need and ask them to do. We double-bind them and trap ourselves; and community does not happen. We are satisfied to become a conglomerate of opinionated loners, who periodically try and even torture one another with our sophistries. We hope that community can happen logically or rationally so that we can avoid the compassionate and vulnerable life. We are still dealing with the first, most all-pervasive, and best disguised sin of all: the pride that keeps us from depending on another.

Perhaps we can be aided through this obstacle course by one essential insight: The power is not finally in the leader but in the group. The authority is in the leader, and that authority is precisely the ability to recognize, affirm, and tap the power of the group. When a person can release and integrate that power for the good of the group, he or she will be a founder or leader of some aspect of community.

This charism of community authorship seems to be even rarer than the gift of leadership itself. Many people are at least leading people to grow, but few are leading people to grow together. The latter is the pastoral function of the church, which is rare simply because for the most part it has not been expected.

When leaders can no longer tap the power of the group, they will no longer lead. They might hold a role or office or even a sacred ordination, but they will not be leading unless others are freely following; their authority is not authoring other people.

This kind of leadership only destroys and discourages others' experience of their own power. A good authority will always give a group and individuals a deep sense of this power.

Good leadership, therefore, is not simply having good ideas or the ability to exercise control but having the ability to love deeply and believe in other people. Thus, as Jesus said from the beginning, leadership is the truest kind of servanthood, and its job is to listen rather than to speak, to hope rather than to enforce.

Inner authority becomes external authority when it both comes from within and simultaneously attracts, affirms, and directs others. This is almost too much to hope for in one human being. Human history, even church history, has become so despairing of ever expecting it that we have settled for authoritarian leaders to fill the gap. And these often must be authoritarian precisely because they are not authoritative. They are not in touch with deep human truth.

The powers of the world, who are always fighting time deadlines, management goals, and profit scales, do not expect to be motivated from within. They cannot afford to be, lest people seek truth instead of control. But we who seek to build the earth in the image of God—what about us?

The author of life bids us share in his freedom and authority. This will take longer, but it will also last longer; and this God seems to be building for the long haul. God waits, as only God can wait, because he knows that he is God. Those with true authority can believe because they know that they know. And the rose can both blossom and die because she knows that she is a rose.

5

TO CARE AND NOT TO CARE

The Future of Religious Life

In reflecting on the future and renewal of religious life, I have found clear guidance in some words from T. S. Eliot's poem "Ash Wednesday." At the end of the long poem, he concludes with these lines:

> Spirit of the fountain; spirit of the garden,
> Suffer us not to mock ourselves with falsehood
> Teach us to care and not to care
> Teach us to sit still
> Even among these rocks,
> Our peace in His will
> And even among these rocks . . .

If there is one spiritual discipline that I believe will be necessary for the refounding of Western religious life, it is a renewed appreciation for the necessity of detachment. I have seen much havoc played out in our lives and ministries by what I would call "an excess of caring." Not necessarily a benevolent caring for issues of others, but an undue and compulsive attachment to our own ideas, our own feelings, our own opinions, just because they are our own. Sometimes it seems that is the only ego identity that many people have. I am my feelings. I have a feeling which must be shared and received. And it all too quickly becomes "My feelings have me." Soon there is no way out of the morass of subjectivity, and religious life itself can become a largely interpersonal and therapeutic society that merely echoes the larger society instead of providing an honest and restful alternative to it.

I am convinced that the form of liberation theology for our First World context must be a form of liberation from the tyranny of emotions, the tyranny of psychic preoccupations, the tyranny of the separate, individually bound ego. Any structures, formation programs, community models that continue to equate religious life with the modern therapeutic society will only be regressive and confirm some of the worst aspects of an overly narcissistic society. It will prepare us for many future religious who will be preoccupied with self-help instead of service, fixing the psyche instead of the much more demanding journey to their contemplative center. Pelagian and semi-Pelagian techniques (*"I* must make it happen!"*) instead of the much more traditional teachings on positive detachment and spiritual surrender.

I am aware that these words can be highly misconstrued as dualistic or anti-psychological. But that is not my point. Quite the contrary. I am convinced that we have access to an authentic spiritual level ("the soul," the true self, the contemplative center, who I am in God before I do anything or anything is done to me) that is previous and foundational to all issues of parenting, woundedness, dysfunction and "what I feel." It is of crucial importance for the future of our religious communities that we be and be seen as people who merely use the wonderful psychological tools of our culture to serve and deepen our radical position at a spiritual center. Far too often, even among very good and dedicated people, I see that the overbearing influence of our therapeutic society has turned it around: Spirituality seems to be serving the psychological person instead of psychology serving the movement toward union, surrender, trust, and what I think is holiness.

I know there is a very good and helpful meaning to the phrase "Holiness is wholeness," but it is also the luxurious thinking of an affluent culture and is very often just not true. I know too many broken and neurotic religious (myself!) who often, because of their brokenness, have learned how to collapse back into the center, rely upon the mercy, discover the wellsprings of the Compassionate One.

What I am trying to say is that for religious life to be an alternative to our society it must be clear what we are rejecting. We have become afraid of that word in the post-Vatican II era of the "secular city." I am often afraid that this is the large nucleus of truth that many reactionary types have against the renewal of church forms. Our embracings have not been clarified and balanced by our rejections, and so the world is unsure as to what our real corporate values are. The conservative element then moves away from integration, because we ourselves have not integrated.

Clearly, the biblical and religious-life tradition is saying that the false self of ego, security, careerism, privatized self-development, is a tremendous danger to the emergence of the authentic soul. An encounter with the Absolute is always an experience of death for the private self. I find, however, that the necessary questioning of the world of psychological self-development confronts us with an idol closer to home for most of us who are working for renewal and refounding. We need to name this idol more precisely.

But the goal of detachment is so that we can attach ourselves more passionately. The false self must die so that the true self may emerge. Rejection is for the sake of pure embracing. What is it that we must clearly embrace? Somehow our lives individually and corporately must clearly speak, publicly speak, unashamedly speak of our love of God. Our love of our work, our love of life, our love of people, all speak of this to those who know how to listen.

But in the early stages of religious development, which is where most people are, we must warmly name our Lover. Not just in ritual, not just in proper form and action, not just in aesthetic quote and banner, but personally, one to one, frankly, honestly, with truth and doubt and desire.

Taught by the Poor

The lifestyle choices, the ministry, the words of Jesus make it clear where the gospel is learned: The privileged perspective is from the bottom of society. The primary reformers and original founders of religious life were always women and men who either never lost or somehow rediscovered that perspective. From that position they knew what questions to ask, what issues to ignore and where true power, security, and holiness were to be found. Those at the top of any pile, those enjoying positions of privilege, have too much to protect to ask imaginative questions. "The rich," as Jesus calls them, do not long and thirst for newness. They necessarily fear and fret for the status quo. The life to which they have become accustomed becomes normative and usually narrows their options. This is true in the area of business and economics, politics, education, and also in the area of religion. That is the consistent and proved danger for a professional religious class. It is the danger of creating "the separated ones," "clerics," the clergy.

Religious life, particularly male religious life, must be free to see itself as a mediating and "bottom-heavy" structure within the church. It must be ready whenever possible to take the side of the powerless, the non-clerics, the perspective other than power, law, order, and control. I am convinced that was the social reason for the vow of poverty, the desire of so many brothers' institutes to remain laymen and the wisdom of my own father, St. Francis, in refusing priestly ordination. The wisdom figures seem to have known the danger of the power perspective, at least intuitively. All the groups that wanted to call themselves "minors," "minims," and "little brothers or sisters of something" should be shouting the message very clearly.

Practically and simply put, we need to be in close and immediate contact with the poor—not to help them, not to teach them, not to empower them, not to make Catholics out of them—but so that we ourselves can learn what the appropriate questions are, what to pay attention to, and how to move to our own places of pain and oppression. It is there that God has by far the best chance of getting at us! We need them more than they need us! It's rightly called "reverse mission."

As correct as it sounds, I am sure that Jesus is not primarily calling us to help the poor and the oppressed. If I look at Jesus' own choices, he is much more concerned about liberating the oppressors than liberating the oppressed. Then the problems of the oppressed take care of themselves. He goes to the lepers, the disabled, the prostitute, the disenfranchised for his own companionship and encouragement. Again and again he says, "Never have I found such faith," and "You are whole!" and "Blessed are you!" It would be wrong, however, to say that Jesus never hung around with the wealthy and privileged. In fact he often did and even accepted dinner invitations. But it can be documented point by point that he always challenged them too. We are to be bridge builders, but with the tools and materials of the poor in firm grasp.

Communities of Justice

We must not make our own refounding choices in terms of "How can we (from our position of secure privilege) help the poor (in their inferior position) through works of charity?" Neither the world nor the poor see charity in these decisions anymore, but usually the unconscious perpetuation of injustice and our own spiritual superiority. The world is no longer impressed by charity when it is not built on justice. The world no longer needs or wants our sometimes self-serving charity when it merely covers over or even deepens the social problem. In this case the world's cynicism is also the truth.

The world, and hopefully the church, is ready for communities of justice who have themselves been taught by the poor and can therefore teach and conscienticize the larger world and the unaware church. Only communities of justice will have the authority to speak the gospel to the great social movements of our time. The women, the minorities, the disabled, the homosexuals, the ethnic groupings, the peace movements, have all learned about the nature of social power and domination. They have experienced the institutionalized violence, the hidden violence of patriarchal societies. Thinking and prayerful men and women from these groups are not about to support us or join us if they see us as part of the problem instead of part of the solution. And I don't think they should.

In maintaining communities of "charity" and service that are not built on justice, we are still part of the old principalities and powers that Jesus came to get rid of "and drag behind him in his great triumphal procession" (Colossians 1:15). Our country is becoming too sophisticated not to recognize the difference between secure self-interest and genuine servanthood. Again, I would suggest that this is the historical and consistent social meaning of the vow of poverty. This will probably sound very Franciscan, but for an economically obsessed capitalist culture like our own, a refounded religious life is going to have to name and exorcise the money demon very clearly and deliberately. The spiritually aware will not let us get away with anything less, and they are the ones we must attract to our lifestyle if we are to continue evangelizing this American culture. Which brings me to my next point.

Evangelization of Culture

Our culture speaks an unconscious and uncritical language of individualism. We are often not even aware that there is another way to talk, another way to think, another way to pray. We are for the most part unaware, even Catholics and especially younger American Catholics, that there is a "second language" that is still used by communities of memory and hope. There is an alternative to whimsical "lifestyle enclaves" built on feelings and individual development. The great Catholic synthesis that probably reached its peak in the thirteenth century still believed in the principle of the common good, still believed that its forms of religious life were a second language that spoke clearly not just to individual souls, but to the soul of society itself.

I would suspect that whichever of our communities are able to pass through this crisis of refoundation, these groups will have seen themselves—and be seen—as vehicles of cultural good news. They will speak to the age and the moment and not just to the individual's role in the church or to personal growth and secure belonging. Secure belonging systems will always be attractive to those with a weak sense of identity, those who are not self-starters, those who are passive and passive-aggressive, those who never had a family or came from a dysfunctional family. My guess would be that we will be overwhelmed by such members in the decades ahead if we continue to over-present ourselves as places of warm belonging, secure role and individual opportunity.

Of course, there is such a thing as fully legitimate and necessary self-interest, but we had better not appeal to it in the first instance. Honesty poses the question whether that is not what we have been doing for most of this century and why we have so many disaffected, unmotivated, and passive members today. If that sad observation is to be made, I guess I am most free to make it as a male religious myself—and there is no group that is more ready to know it and talk about it than this very group.

As to what we mean by the evangelization of culture, I can do nothing better than again quote the hero of the Second Vatican Council, Pope Paul VI:

For the church it is a question not only of preaching the Gospel in ever-wider geographic areas or to ever-greater numbers of people, but also of affecting, and as it were upsetting, through the power of the Gospel, humanity's criteria of judgment, determining values, points of interest, lines of thought, sources of inspiration and models of life, which are in contrast with the word of God and the plan of salvation. All this could be expressed in the following words: What matters is to evangelize human culture and cultures, not in a purely decorative way, as it were by applying a thin veneer, but in a vital way, in depth and right to their very roots. (*Evangelii Nuntiandi*, 19-20)

This is a task that is uniquely carried by community and particularly by communities of memory and hope that are grounded in the past and drawn to the future. An individual is not adequate to the task and will be marginalized as eccentric, uneducated, unpatriotic, and invisible. In a certain and very real sense, religious life is more geared to this task of corporate evangelization than the church itself.

After many years of retreats to both diocesan and religious priests, it is obvious to me that we religious are freer by reason of structure and jurisdiction (and sometimes formation) to see the bigger picture. In the Catholic Church the radical new vision does not have to separate and form an Amish or Quaker denomination; we form a religious order within the great mother church. But if we, the religious, end up preaching and living a merely cultural gospel of civil religion, what leaven for renewal will there be? "If the salt loses its taste, who will salt the salt?" (Matthew 5:13). Or as Luke puts it, "Make sure that the light you have to offer is not in fact darkness" (Luke 11:35).

Our job is not just to do good, it is to do good together. Our job is not just to be good, it is to be the common good. Our job is not just to announce good news to persons, it is to announce a new reality where it will be possible for persons to do the good, to be good. Our structures must speak of a communal liberation where people can be spiritually imaginative, politically risky, and where good news is visible for all, especially for the poor and oppressed. Any other structures point to our own self-interest rather than God's reign.

The Rules of Union

We all know that union is the goal, but for some reason it has not been so obvious that union must also be the means. Look at our failure to recognize the clear nonviolent teaching of Jesus, his teaching on love of enemies, forgiveness and compassion. There were always situations where it did not apply. Again internal resistance was not named, and self-will again held sway. For the Christian the first and final rule is always love. This is not necessarily soft love, but a recognition that there is no love lost in the world, and our job is to put it out, hard or soft, not asking the question of worthiness or risk, and let God take it from there.

The world of love, its stages, its disguises, its counterfeits, its forms, its energies, its goals, its godliness, its demons, are surely the most important course of study we will ever take in this world. And for one who desires to communicate Christ and to seek union with Christ, it is a course that we cannot skip out on in the name of church career or formal celibacy.

I can do no more here than raise the question: I believe in the charism of celibacy. I have seen it bear fruit for the church and for many individuals who truly have the charism or have begged for the grace. We also know many celibates whose lives have not been at all happy or fruitful for anybody. Others may make the statistical percentages. I wouldn't dare.

But is there a form of celibate religious life that will necessitate learning the rules of love and union? Is there a form of life that will not pander to the misogynist, those afraid of intimacy, the self-seeking homosexual, those who do not want to be bothered by children, family, and personal responsibility? In my experience on priests' retreats as confessor and spiritual director, I think I can say these three things: The happiest and healthiest celibates I know have consistently and not always "successfully" risked intimacy. Second, the happiest and healthiest tend to have ongoing and in-depth relationships with Christian families as families. Third, and it probably includes the first two, they have found some way to meet the human need for tactility and personal warmth. I would stand before the pope and say that outside of this group I meet largely unhappy, non-generative or even neurotic personalities. Maybe my experience is wrong, but I must risk sharing it. It's all I have.

Our refounding must find a spirituality that includes lay and religious bonding, or better, family and celibate relationships that allow in-depth friendship, prayer, struggle, and forgiveness. I do not know any other way that we will learn the rules of union. The basic ecclesial team which I continue to see as most life-giving is the partnership of celibates and married couples. We see it in St. Paul himself, with Priscilla and Aquila, we see it in the base communities of Latin America, we see it in Marriage and Engaged Encounter, and I have had the privilege of living it long term both at New Jerusalem Community in Cincinnati and at the Center for Action and Contemplation in Albuquerque, where a central couple shares and supports my work in every way.

Lest my point be lost — and I know it has many daring implications — religious who spend their whole life "in house" with their own gender-safe groups are not by and large the religious whom I see as alive role models for the coming age. Far too often their shadow is so denied, their social skills so poor, their vulnerability so untested that they have to move farther and farther into isolation as life progresses. That cannot be the salvation that God is offering. We must refound the meaning of the vow of celibate chastity. The world knows nothing about purity, but sometimes we know nothing about passion. We must teach one another.

The Vocation of Spiritual Friendship

In a culture which recognizes, articulates and supports only two kinds of public role in the world — job and career — we must refound and articulate the third, which is vocation. It must be clear to ourselves and to this culture that we are about something different and something more than job and career. We must refound it on a level deeper than the therapeutic, deeper than the functional or practical, deeper than charity or service works, deeper than helpful belonging systems or happy lifestyle enclaves.

Just as Aristotle, Cicero, and Aquinas recognized the necessity of a third level of true friendship, "a common commitment to the common good," so I do not suspect religious life can refound itself in this culture of utilitarianism and self-interest unless it recommits itself not just to what works and what helps but to what is. This is, of course, a recommitment to the spiritual search, to the contemplative center, to a place of spiritual objectivity, a place of common and individual goodness beyond the merely psychic, beyond the primary weighing of feelings, beyond what is good for me right now, beyond American cultural biases, and yes, even beyond "What's good for the Roman Catholic Church is good for the kingdom."

The common good is the totally common good and leaves none of our sacred cows protected in the pen. If the kingdom is absolute, then all else is relative. As Jesus puts it, all else is "the rest," which will be given to us "besides" (Matthew 6:33). Religious life must first of all be kingdom life before it is too quickly a matter of church jobs. That is its objectivity and ground.

Ours is a vocation and therefore cannot be tied closely to the usual rewards of power, prestige, or possessions. These speak of job, career, convenient belonging system; Jesus warns strongly against them because they more than anything else tend to blind us to kingdom values and tie us up in the same system as everybody else. Only the words are different.

Of course, I have not provided all the answers. But I do hope these reflections might at least help to stir the Spirit and awaken the unconscious to some Gospel imagination. I would hope that it might at least help us to overcome hopelessness or neutrality. Neutrality will always serve the status quo. Gospel will always serve the future of hope. Why else are all of these visions and desires stirring in the hearts of men and women from even fifth- and thirteenth-century communities? Refounding must be possible and desirable or the good Lord would not play such games with our hearts. To follow the lines of John Duns Scotus' argument for the Immaculate Conception—with a bit of liberty—"If it is possible, and it is fitting, then it will be done." Our feeble minds say it is possible, our crushed hearts feel it to be fitting, and now we ask God to let it be done—even through us.

> Spirit of the fountain; spirit of the garden,
> Suffer us not to mock ourselves with falsehood
> Teach us to care and not to care
> Teach us to sit still
> Even among these rocks,
> Our peace in His will
> And even among these rocks . . .

A LIFE PURE AND SIMPLE

Reflections on St. Francis of Assisi

Beauty hurts, especially for those who have once seen how beautiful it really is. Ugliness irritates, but only for those who have never seen. When the great seers arise, their lives always confuse the rest of us. They seem to change all the rules, look in different directions for joy, and find love in the most unsuspected places.

Those who have seen the full extent of beauty set our minds awhirl; we take centuries to rediscover our bearings, and meanwhile, chase blinking-eyed after them. Such a seer was Francisco Bernardone (1182-1226), and such a people is that admiring and unsettled portion of humanity that for 800 years has been unable to forget what he saw and what he did with his one little life. His beauty and his seeing still hurt us.

More than any other follower of Christ, Francis of Assisi has been called a "second Christ." More lives have been written of him than of any other person except Jesus himself. He has been the most painted non-biblical character in history, and the usually cautious church declared him a saint only four years after his death. G. K. Chesterton called him "the world's one quite sincere democrat," and the "first hero of humanism."

Lenin spoke enviously of him shortly before he died, and Sir Kenneth Clark called him Europe's greatest religious genius. Even in his own lifetime he exerted a strange attractiveness. Perhaps it was the undeniable magnetism that occurs when truth and folly stand together:

> One day when St. Francis was coming back from the woods, where he had been praying, and was at the edge of the forest, Brother Masseo went to meet him, and said to St. Francis, half-jokingly, "Why after you? Why after you? Why after you? Why does all the world seem to be running after you, and everyone seems to want to see you and hear you and obey you? You are not a handsome man. You do not have great learning or wisdom. You are not a nobleman. So why is all the world running after you?"
>
> Then with great fervor of spirit he turned to Brother Masseo and said: "You want to know why after me? You really want to know why everyone is running after me? I have this from the all-holy eyes of God that see the good and the evil everywhere. For those blessed and all-holy eyes have not seen among sinners anyone more vile or insufficient than I am. And so in order to do that wonderful work which he intends to do, he did not find on earth a more ordinary creature, and therefore he chose me. For God has chosen the foolish things of this world to put to shame the wise, and God has chosen the base things of this world and the despised, to bring to naught the noble, the great and the strong."
>
> *The Little Flowers of St. Francis*

Francis' starting place was utter truth. His prayer for nights on end was simply: "Who are you, O God? And who am I?" He repeated it without ceasing, and the above response seems to be his answer. He knew that he was radically unfinished and that he always would be. As he charted his own conversion to the moment when he could embrace an ugly and smelly leper, so his journey in truth began when he could accept the leper part of himself. He spent much of the rest of his life not hiding or disguising that truth, but actually seeming to advertise it. This deep acceptance of his own limitations and capacity for evil had none of the destructiveness and self-loathing that we often find in ourselves. He only rejoiced in the possibility and promise of their redemption.

Francis' reading of the gospel is of utmost relevance today. His focus and emphasis is the same as Jesus'. His life was an enacted parable, an audio-visual aid to gospel freedom. It gives us the perspective by which to see as Jesus did: the view from the bottom. He insists by every facet of his life that we can only see rightly from a dis-established position. He wanted to be poor first of all simply because Jesus was poor. But he also knew that the biblical promises were made to the poor, that the gospel could be preached only to the poor because they alone had the freedom to hear it without distorting it for their own purposes. He wanted to have nothing to protect except the love which made all else useless. "Love is not loved! Love is not loved!" he used to sigh.

Contrary to the rest of the human race, therefore, he raced in the other direction, certain that he was following the path of Christ. Like Paul, all he wanted was "to know Christ and the power of his resurrection and to share his sufferings by reproducing the pattern of his death" (Philippians 3:11). He knew there was no life in the secure life at the top. He himself had begun there as the son of a rich cloth merchant, and he saw that much of the church had been seduced and entrapped into a kind of spiritual materialism, all the more illusory because it appeared to be for the sake of God and the work of the kingdom. He often referred to himself as an "*idiota*," but he was not so stupid as to be unable to recognize simple freedom and the lack of it.

Francis never wanted to write a rule, or code of behavior, for his friars, despite the insistence of Rome. He was always quite satisfied with Jesus' Sermon on the Mount and his instructions

metaphysics

to the disciples. When they finally convinced him that he r
write a rule, he simply connected a series of gospel quotes
together with his own admonitions. This remains the rule of
the Friars Minor to this day, and was somewhat grudgingly
approved by Pope Honorius III in the year 1223.

When Francis read the inaugural discourse of Jesus, he saw
that the call to be poor stood right at the beginning: "How
happy are the poor!" Henceforward, Francis' reading of the
gospel considered poverty to be "the foundation of all other
virtues and their guardian." The other virtues receive the kingdom only in promise; poverty, however, is invested with it
already now and without delay. "Theirs is the kingdom of
heaven" (Matthew 5:3).

As a result, Franciscan spirituality has never been an abstraction. It is grounded in Jesus' specific instructions to his disciples and not in theology. It is not easily able to move into
ideology or to hide behind denominational screens into which
we have projected our own metaphysics. Francis' living of the
gospel was just that: It was lifestyle pure and simple. It was
the incarnation continuing in space and time. It was the presence of the Spirit taken absolutely seriously. It was being Jesus
more than simply worshiping him. At its best, Franciscanism is
not words or even ethics. It is flesh—naked flesh—unable to
deny its limitations, unable to cover its wounds. He called it
poverty.

This pure vision of gospel life attracted thousands to a new
freedom in the church and in ministry. Religious communities
had become more and more entangled with stipends, benefices,
and rich land holdings. Members lived individually simple lives
but were corporately secure and even comfortable. The beg-
ging, or mendicant, orders were born to break that dangerous
marriage between ministry and money. Francis did not want
his friars to preach salvation (although they did that too) as
much as he wanted them to be salvation. He wanted them to
model and image the life of Jesus in the world, with all of the
trusting and insecurity that that would entail. Today we would

be arrested as vagrants or bums, but he believed that Jesus meant what he said when he told the disciples to "eat whatever is set before you, for the laborer deserves his wages" (Luke 10:7). When Francis first heard Jesus' sermon in which he told his followers to "take nothing for your journey," he left Mass overjoyed, and committed the whole passage to memory, saying "This is what I want. This is what I long for. This is what I desire to do with all my heart."

When I think of the life of Francis, I am reminded of a poor Lutheran pastor and his wife whom I met in a small village in Germany. When he left the room, she spoke of her husband with great love and respect even though his radical commitment to the gospel had brought her great pain and privation. Before he re-entered, she whispered to me solemnly and proudly, "He makes being poor look brilliant! And like brilliance, he lights up everything." So also Francis was no dark ascetic, but a passionate and sensuous Italian, who did not equate poverty with gracelessness or slovenliness. One need only visit his prayer spots throughout central Italy to discover that he chose the most scenic and lovely settings in which to disclose the darkness of his own soul. He knew that he had to surround himself with God's delighting in order to risk such painful truths.

Francis could not just be poor; he had to have a love affair and even a marriage with his beloved, "Lady Poverty." His celibacy had to be a passion, not a lack of it. In the twelfth-century tradition of courtly love, the sublimated love of a knight for his idealized lady, Francis insisted that he would marry only "the noblest, the richest, the most beautiful woman ever seen." She turned out to be Lady Poverty.

> The blessed father considered the common wealth of the sons of men as trifles, and ambitious for higher things, he longed for Lady Poverty with all his heart. Looking upon poverty as especially dear to the Son of God, though it was spurned throughout the whole world, he sought to

espouse it in perpetual charity. Therefore, after he had become a lover of her beauty, he not only left his father and mother, but even put aside all things that he might cling to her more closely as his spouse and that they might be two in one spirit. . . . There was no one so desirous of gold as he was desirous of poverty, and no one so solicitous in guarding his treasure as he was solicitous in guarding this pearl of the gospel.

Thomas of Celano, *Second Life*

Francis was enough of a realist to know that this view from the bottom would never become fashionable. Yet his commitment to littleness led him to name his brothers "minors" so that they would never fall back again into the worldview of the "majors" (the great, the nobility). He knew that there was power in being a somebody, but that there was truth in being a nobody. He always opted for the truth, and from the example of Jesus crucified knew that the Lord would create power out of that. He was astonishingly unimpressed by numbers, success, degrees, status symbols, and even clerical ordination, which he refused. He was not about to be coopted by any kingdoms less than that of the "Great King." He never railed against the show and trappings of medieval Catholicism; he simply moved outside the walls of Assisi and did it in a new way. He knew that frontal attacks never work anyway, and he loved the church too much to presume to judge the others. Again, it was his lifestyle which shouted judgment, not his words. He was a gentle prophet. His witness, therefore, has been able to call and challenge believers for eight centuries.

Francis' choice of weakness instead of strength, vulnerability instead of righteousness, truth instead of practicality, honesty instead of influence stands in amazing contrast to the general Westernized version of the gospel, and to the success-oriented and electronic church so readily received today. He is forever the saint of "holy topsy-turveydom," as G. K. Chesterton said.

Francis seemed to have very little conscious awareness of

what we would today call corporate or systemic evil. At least
he did not consciously speak of his mission in that light. Yet if
his interpretation of the gospel had been taken as foundational
instead of merely admired and then marginalized, one can only
imagine the different color and character of Western Christianity and civilization today. If greed and power and control had
been recognized as the demons they are, if spiritual goods could
have been fittingly valued, the Renaissance could have been
for real, the Reformation might not have been necessary, the
Enlightenment could have moved beyond the mind and the
subjective, and the class warfare called for by Marxism would
not have been necessary. Because most of the church has
refused to take Jesus' teaching and Francis' example seriously,
now much of the world refuses to take us seriously. "Your Christianity is all in the head," they say. "You Christians love to talk
of a new life, but the record shows that you are afraid to live
in a new way—a way that is responsible, caring, and making for
peace."

Living in a feudal period of history, Francis had no knowledge of the monstrous proportions that our love of war would
attain, but in his own limited world, he abandoned his early life as a knight and warrior, even though this career was
very esteemed and culturally approved. He applied that same
knightly chivalry and courage to the local battles for goodness.
In their greeting the Friars Minor were to announce their purpose:

> "The Lord revealed to me that I should say as a greeting,
> 'The Lord give you peace.'" And one day when he was
> traveling with a friar who was one of the first twelve, he
> used to greet people along the road and in the fields with
> his greeting of peace. And because people had never heard
> such a greeting from any religious, they were very startled.
> Indeed, some said indignantly, "What do you mean by
> this greeting of yours?" As a result the friar became
> embarrassed, and said to Francis, "Allow us to use some

other greetings." But the holy father said, "Let them chatter, for they do not understand the ways of God. Don't feel ashamed because of this, for one day the nobles and princes of this world will respect you and the other friars for this greeting. For it is no marvel if the Lord should desire to have a new little flock, whose speech and way of life are unlike those of all its predecessors, and which is content to possess him alone."

The Mirror of Perfection

And centuries later the church is still calling forth embarrassingly little flocks to speak the gospel of peace, while the nobles and princes of this world are still withholding their respect. The saints of every age must learn to trust only in eschatological victories.

Perhaps no one understood the vision and vocation of Francis better than a young, wealthy woman of Assisi named Clare Scifi (1194-1253). She took the call of gospel poverty to her heart like no other. Of Francis she said, "After God he is the charioteer of my soul." She received from Innocent III in 1216 and from Gregory IX in 1228 her famous "Privilege of Poverty." It took two papal pronouncements to protect and assure a religious community that they would be allowed to live in insecurity. Clare knew that wise and prudent people would try to take away what she saw as essential to gospel life.

It is generally agreed that the female branch of the Franciscan family has likely lived the poverty and contemplation of Francis much more faithfully than have the friars. Many reasons could probably be given for this, but the most obvious is that the men have been used for religious function and jurisdiction in the institutional church, which invariably takes away one's appreciation of lifestyle as an end in itself. The friars were inserted into the power structure where they could no longer view life from the edge or from below, but had to maintain the system. Unfortunately, the "Poor Clares" have had to remain in a cloister to retain their privileged vantage point. Maybe there is no other way. History has shown us how rare it is for people to be both in the world and yet not of the world, as Jesus has called us. Even though few seem to attain this balance, it will always remain the Franciscan ideal.

Franciscans have usually been seen as "of the people." Our self-image is one of "blue-collar clergy" instead of white-collar or Roman-collar professionals. This has allowed the friars to be in closer touch with the concerns of ordinary folk, but sometimes out of touch with good and corrective thinking. As always, one's gift is one's liability. The friars have often reflected the common folks' prejudices and fears as much as they have reflected their concerns for justice and compassion.

Francis saw himself as a reconciler and preacher of forgiveness. After a long-standing quarrel between the mayor and the bishop of Assisi, he decided to add another verse to his famous "Canticle of Brother Sun." Even here there was no room in his spacious heart for harsh epithets or cruel judgments. He had seen too much beauty. He hurt when others hurt. And even his reconciliations took the form of art and courtesy, in what is considered to be the first piece of Italian poetry.

> "It is a great shame for us, the servants of God, that at a time when the mayor and the bishop so hate each other no one can be found to re-establish peace and concord between them," said Francis to his companions. And so he added a further strophe to his Canticle of Brother Sun:
> All praise be yours, my Lord,
> Through those who grant pardon for love of you;
> Through those who endure trial and persecution.
> Happy those who endure in peace;
> By you, Most High, they will be crowned.
> And the friars went to the Piazza Commune and sang the full canticle in the presence of the mayor and the bishop. And with much tenderness and affection they both locked arms and embraced each other.
>
> *The Legend of Perugia*

In the times of Francis "not only had war and its orgies and disorders become a necessity and a habit, but they had become the preferred occupation, the ruling passion, and the whole life of the city, in which 'peace' no longer had any meaning" (*Nova Vita*). Undoubtedly the most famous of Francis' ventures into peacemaking was his personal visit with the sultan, Melek-el-Khamil (1217-1238) at Damietta in Egypt. He had made several previous trips to crusaders camps in Syria, and had been turned back by sickness and shipwreck. This time the crusaders had been fighting since May 9 of 1218 until the very day of August 29, 1219, when Francis arrived in Egypt. He spent several days with the sultan trying to arrange a peace, but only gained his personal respect. He turned then to the Christian crusaders:

"If I tell them to fight, I will be considered a fool; if I am silent I will not escape my conscience." And so the holy man arose and approached the Christians with salutary warnings, forbidding the war, denouncing the reasons for it. But truth was turned to ridicule, and they hardened their heart and refused to be guided. They went, they joined battle, they fought and our (sic) army was pressed hard by the enemy. So great was the number of soldiers lost in the disaster that six thousand were among the dead and captured. Compassion pressed upon the holy man, even though they were not regretful over the deed. He mourned especially over the Spaniards, when he saw how their great impetuosity had left but a few of them remaining. Let the princes of this world know these things and let them know that it is not easy to fight against God, against the will of the Lord. Rashness generally ends in disaster, for it relies on its own power and does not deserve help from heaven. But if victory is to be hoped for from on high, battles must be entrusted to the Spirit of God.

Second Life

Unfortunately, history tells us that fighting resumed on September 26, and Francis returned to Assisi a very discouraged man. Yet his warnings to his followers are apt for peacemakers and those working for justice in our day:

> "While you are proclaiming peace with your lips, be careful to have it even more fully in your heart. Nobody should be roused to wrath or insult on your account. Everyone should rather be moved to peace, goodwill, and mercy as a result of your self-restraint. For we have been called for the purpose of healing the wounded, binding up those who are bruised, and reclaiming the erring."
>
> *The Legend of the Three Companions*

Many historians consider Francis' rule of life for lay people one of the major contributing factors to the death of feudalism. Feudalism was a system based on oppression and control. Feuds and vendettas were so common that few people went abroad unarmed. Yet Francis forbade his followers to fight, carry weapons, or even swear allegiance to any noble. Again this was based in Jesus' teaching from the Sermon on the Mount. So many thousands of people committed themselves to this "Third Order rule" that it was one of the world's few successful social revolutions, even if rather short-lived.

Despite all of his legitimate reasons for discouragement, Francis was known as a man of deep and abiding joy. He knew that after all was done and undone, he was still "the herald of the Great King." No one should ever doubt that Francis was quintessentially a man in love, and a man in love with the greatest of lovers. There was simply no bottom to his grateful happiness. He told his friars that it was their vocation "to lift up people's hearts and give them reasons for spiritual joy." They needed no other justification for their life. They needed no other ministry in the church. They, like he, were to be troubadours and minstrels of the Lord. At times, eyewitnesses tell us that he was so filled with gladness that "he would pick up a stick from the ground and putting it over his left arm, would draw across it, as across a violin, a little bow bent by means of a string; and going through the motions of playing, he would sing about the Lord. This whole ecstasy of joy would often end in tears and would be dissolved in compassion" (*Second Life*). To communicate this wisdom of the heart to his community, he engaged Brother Leo in one of his most quoted stories, the dialogue of perfect joy:

> One winter day when he and Brother Leo were walking along the road to Assisi from Perugia, Francis called out to Leo in the bitter cold five times, each time telling him what perfect joy was not: "Brother Leo, even if a Friar Minor gives sight to the blind, heals the paralyzed, drives out devils, gives hearing back to the deaf, makes the lame walk, and restores speech to the dumb, and what is more brings back to life a man who has been dead four days, write that perfect joy is not in that." And so he continued with different enumerations of success and even spiritual enjoyment. And when he had been talking this way for a distance of two miles, Brother Leo in great amazement asked him: "Father, I beg you in God's name to tell me where perfect joy is to be found?"
>
> And Francis replied: "When we come to the Portiuncula, soaked by the rain and frozen by the cold, all soiled with mud and suffering from hunger, and we ring at the gate of our friary and the brother porter comes and says angrily: 'Who are you?' And we say: 'We are two of your brothers.' And he contradicts us, saying, 'You are not telling the truth, Go away!' And he does not open for us, but makes us stand outside in the snow and rain, cold and hungry until night falls—then if we endure all of those insults and cruel rebuffs patiently, without being troubled and without complaining, and if we reflect humbly and lovingly that the porter really knows us. Oh Brother Leo, write that perfect joy is to be found there!

"And if we continue to knock and the porter comes out
and drives us away with curses and hard blows — and if we
bear it patiently and take the insults with joy and love in
our hearts. Oh, Brother Leo, write down that that is perfect joy! And now hear the conclusion: Above all the graces
and gifts of the Holy Spirit which Christ gives to his
friends is that of conquering oneself and willingly enduring sufferings, insults, humiliations, and hardships for the
love of Christ."

The Little Flowers of St. Francis

This is not so much a description of perfect joy as it is a
description of perfect freedom. Here at last we have a truly
nonviolent and liberated man. Only such as these will ever
liberate others. They are not part of the problem, but most
assuredly the beginnings of the solution. They have moved
beyond here and there, mine and yours, beyond all manner of
divisions, to recognize the "dearest freshness, deep down
things" (G. M. Hopkins). They seem to accept without despair
that we are together in one another's sin, and they seem to
honestly enjoy one another's glories. Every part really is trying
to love every other part — but with great struggle and obstacles
unlimited. Some few people become points where all the parts
can meet. And these rare jigsaw pieces of persons hold the rest
of the puzzled picture together. They give us both cause for
sanity and excuses for outrageous adventure. But to do that for
us they must become small enough so that none of us is threat-
ened, so that we can think we are actually giving instead of
receiving.

These free ones must be the rejoicing of God. These few
tell us what is going on inside the heart of God. These few
reassure us that whoever this Creator is, God is most assuredly
not omnipotence but humility, not lordly (as God should be)
but infinitely accessible, not withholding but relentlessly wel-
coming. And in their flesh they try to imitate him in an amaz-

ingly un-utopian way, because they are ready to live it in any circumstances whatsoever.

For those like Francis of Assisi goodness has come to be expected, goodness is no surprise, goodness always finally happens, goodness seems to be willing to suffer in order to win, but win it does. For these few free ones, goodness is just there, everywhere, right beneath the surface and quite often breaking through. They cannot resist it nor totally possess it. So they adore. And because they have bowed down, the ugliness of life can attract them, and the beauty of it all is a strange and sacred hurt.

❦ 7 ❦

NEAR OCCASIONS OF GRACE

UTTERLY DIFFERENT AND EXACTLY
THE SAME

The days of life continue to be given. Someone is giving them. All I know for sure is that I am born and merely a small part of a much greater birth. It is enough for a lifetime of wonder.

And that is what it has been. Born into a working-class family in the middle of the Second World War in a small Kansas town, I was unprepared for the life that would follow. Yet forty-seven years later, I know that I am both utterly different and exactly the same as that little boy whom I now remember as a distant but special friend. Who is the Master Worker who has put my life together with such sleight of hand? This God is both my source and my goal, someone I must meet although I am convinced it will be as much a recognition as a discovery. The evidence is around and within me. And the faith to seek and love this mysterious God feels like the same faith that drives me to seek and love myself. Someone is finding me. And I am in wonder.

No matter what religion or denomination we are raised in, our spirituality comes from our life experience. The great Traditions only give name, shape, and ultimate direction to

94

what our heart knows from other sources. This is not new or unorthodox but exactly what Paul said to the Romans: "Ever since God created the world, God's everlasting power and divinity—however invisible—have been there for the mind to see in the things of creation." Similarly, as the Old Testament said, "It is not beyond your strength or beyond your reach. It is not in the heavens, so that you need to ask, 'Who will go up to heaven and bring it down to us?' Nor it is beyond the seas, so that you need to ask, 'Who will cross the seas and bring it back to us?' No, the Word is very near to you, it is in your mouth and in your heart" (Deuteronomy 30:11-14). We must honor the infinite mystery of our own life's journey to recognize God in it. Or is it the other way around? It seems that God is not going to let us get close unless we bring all of ourselves—in love—including our brokenness. That's why the Good News really is good news. Nothing is wasted.

If I do have an ordered theology, I guess a secure childhood would be its beginning and foundation: reality can be trusted. The core is good. Despite all evidence to the contrary, what is is OK. As our Franciscan Doctor, St. Bonaventure, put it, "Being and Goodness are the same thing. They differ only by reason of words." That affirmation is not logically or even psychologically obvious. It is a gift of grace. Some call it faith, some call it hope, and some call it love. But it is surely the beginning of the spiritual journey. The Catholic Tradition calls these the theological virtues, which mean that both their source and their goal are the same—God. These virtues are not worked for, chosen, or achieved. They are given to those who ask, wait, and expect. Until that foundational faith, hope, and love are received, most religion is a disguise, pretense, or a waste of time, more part of the problem than part of the solution.

Until God has elicited that primordial act of confidence in ourselves, in others, in the natural world, it is actually a dodge and a deception to talk about having confidence in God-out-there. The words have no concrete meaning, and religion will only lead us to various forms of legalism, pharisaism, and fear,

ur basic lack of confidence in anything or anybody.
ne piece. You cannot be cynical about yourself and
God, because you really have not gone to the
teaches confidence: the world of adversity. You cannot love anyone unless you learn how to love everyone. Loving, as opposed to liking, is a gift of God's pure being, not called forth by some and withheld from others. It simply is and has nothing to do with the object meeting our needs. Hope is not occasioned by things working out as we expected. If our hope rises or falls according to circumstances, we do not have hope. As Paul says so well in Romans, "We can be happy right now. Our trials produce endurance, and endurance produces a stubborn hope, a hope that will not disappoint us. It is the love of God poured forth in our heart" (5:4-5).

There are two spiritual disciplines that keep me honest and growing: contemplative prayer and the perspective from the bottom. Regarding the first, I was always encouraged in contemplative prayer from my early days as a Franciscan novice. But it was only five years ago that I was freed for a year to pursue that part of my vocation. It was a major turning point. After a thirty-day solitude in Thomas Merton's hermitage in Kentucky, I spent the rest of the year at our Franciscan novitiate house in Cincinnati. I took as my guide a simple phrase: "Don't think. Just look." Father McNamara's definition of contemplation became transformative: "A loving look at the real." The world, my own issues and hurts, all goals and desires gradually dissolved into proper perspective. God became obvious and everywhere.

You see, we do not earn or find God. We just get ourselves out of the way. We let go of illusion and the preoccupations of the false self. As the cheap scaffolding falls away, the soul stands revealed. The soul, or true self, cannot be created or worked for. It is awakened. It is, and it is already. The soul is God's "I AM" continued in me. That part of me already knows, desires, and truly seeks God. That part of me knows how to pray naturally. Here "I" and God seem to be one "I." All we need to do is forget the false self. Don't fight, hate, or reject it. Just observe it and let go of it. As you let go of your own "house" you will find yourself living in a place that is both "utterly different and exactly the same." Merton called it "the palace of nowhere" and Jesus called it "the Father's house." It is the only place you will ever want to live.

I am not there, but I am being urged and led in spite of myself. Someone out there—and within here—is loving me and loving through me. The days continue to be given. And I am in wonder.

NAMING DESPAIR

My early religious training told me that two sins were very heinous and almost unforgivable: presumption and despair. We didn't know then that to disallow too early was actually to allow and empower. By our inability to admit, name, and feel an emotion we had no knowledge that we had it. Now it *has* us— and we are often unaware of its shape, its texture, its energy and power. To condemn too quickly is like destroying one's nerve endings. It keeps one from feeling the pain, but by not feeling the pain, we do not recognize the fire and suffer a much more serious burn. Pain and "sin" are probably our best teachers and our best guardians. We would do better to help people to feel, suffer, and listen to reality than to quickly tell them to avoid it. We are trying to do their homework for them, and we just can't.

The God of Genesis is much wiser:

So from the soil Yahweh God fashioned all the wild beasts and all the birds of heaven. These he brought to Adam to see what he would call them; each one was to bear the name Adam would give it. The man gave names to all the cattle, all the birds of heaven and all the wild beasts. (2:19-20)

God's first act after the creation of Adam, even before the
creation of Eve, was to allow Adam the right to experience and
name his creation, each in its individuality: beasts both domes-
tic and "wild." But we came along later with another idea: We
would spare people the wild beasts. We would unhesitatingly
name them dangerous, bad, *sin*. I once thought this resulted
from the church's benevolent desire for protection and freedom. Now I know that it is much more occasioned by a desire
for control, and even that desire usually proceeds from another
unadmitted emotion: fear.

One of the sad effects of this denial and rejection is a lot of
unrecognized despair in the lives of religious and dedicated
people. It takes the form of low-intensity depression, lack of
basic joy, cynicism, even anger and rage—all because we have
secretly lost hope and refuse to admit it.

Some have seen significant relationships end in divorce or
betrayal; some had expectations of themselves that never came
to pass; many worked for social causes that have only worsened.
Young people joined groups or churches that turned sour or
destructive; many feel the hopelessness of worldwide poverty
and massive militarism, many see structures of meaning, family,
and human relationships collapsing. If you think this despair is
unwarranted or exaggerated, be apprised that a 1940 survey of
public school authorities found that their top discipline problems were "talking, chewing gum, making noise, running in the
halls, getting out of turn in line, dressing improperly, and lit-
tering." A 1986 poll of educators listed "rape, robbery, assault,
burglary, arson, bombings, murder, suicide, drug and alcohol
abuse, gang warfare, pregnancy, abortion, and venereal dis-
eases." There is not only real reason for despair, but one might
ask how aware or concerned someone is who does *not* feel
despair!

But we Christians are people of the resurrection. Don't we
have to be happy and optimistic? That false and superficial
understanding of hope is probably exactly what got us into
denial in the first place. We are condemned, it seems, to feel

the feeling, to walk with our despair. Without doubt, it will reveal the fear, expose the control, move us eventually to a new empowerment—but hurt like hell in the meantime.

In recent decades we have learned that we have to walk through the stages of dying. We have to grieve over lost friends, relatives, and loves. Death cannot be dealt with through quick answers, religious platitudes, or a stiff upper lip. Dying must be allowed to happen, in predictable and necessary stages, in those who die graciously and in those who love them. Elisabeth Kübler-Ross helped us name those stages as denial, anger, bargaining, depression, and finally acceptance.

I suspect that despair is another kind of dying and another kind of pain. It is not so much the loss of persons as the loss of ideals, visions, and plans. For people who hitched their future or their hopes to certain stars, the loss of those stars is experienced as a bitter and disabling movement. It usually happens slowly as we recognize unfulfilled dreams and as we gradually face our own impotence and the "sin of the world" (John 1:29). We are forced to let go of images; images that we built in our youth, images that gave us strength, images that made the future worth living, images that solidified and energized our own self-image. The crash of images is experienced as a death of the spirit, as a loss of hope, as a darkness almost too much to bear. Many, if not most, turn tired and cynical while maintaining the old words that have become clichés even to themselves.

I would describe spiritual growth as the willing surrender of images in favor of the True Image. It is a conversion that never stops, a surrender that never ceases. It is a surrender of self-serving and self-created images of self, of others, of God. Those who worship the images instead of living the Reality simply stop growing spiritually. In this light, the First Commandment takes on a whole new power and poignancy:

> You shall not make yourself a carved image or any likeness
> of anything in heaven or on earth or beneath the earth.
> You shall not bow down before them. (Exodus 20:4-5)

It seems that many people, religious people in particular, would sooner relate to images than to Reality where both despair and God lie hidden.

Until we walk with this despair, we will not know that our hope was hope in ourselves, in our successes, in our power to make a difference, in our image of what perfection and wholeness should be. Until we walk with this despair, we will never uncover the Real Hope on the other side. Until we allow the crash and crush of our images, we will never discover the Real Life beyond what only seems like death. This faith journey is probably the heart of what Jesus came to reveal. It is a pattern not easily known or naturally sought. We call it the Paschal Mystery. It is a constant and yet waiting-to-be-seen pattern: visible and yet invisible like seeds becoming plants (John 12:24).

The hope on the other side of despair is the unique gift of God to those who walk the journey. It is hope not based on anything in particular working out, not based on pie-eyed religious optimism, not based on mind-over-matter determination. It is a hope that comes to those who wait and walk at the same time. It is not just a hope; it is The Hope; a gift not founded on circumstances or successes but a gift that declares that Reality can be trusted after all. Someone is Good somewhere. Goodness is at the beginning and the bottom of all of this. Goodness will win out. Our English language just dropped an *o* and called that Goodness God.

Seek hope. The Hope, on the other side of despair. Waiting and walking with mystery, *faith*, is the only bridge.

RISKING RECONCILIATION

We are both free and trapped by the truth of the gospel. It is *The* Way, and yet the Way that we have not yet taken. It is always calling us to a deeper reliance upon God's mercy, a deeper surrender to that place where we are not in control and do not even have the luxury of knowing we are right. I suspect that is why it is always called "faith" and will always feel like "nothing": nothing we can credit to ourselves, nothing we can take control of, nothing for which we can even condemn ourselves. If true reconciliation is a rare Christian event today, it is because faith is also rare. We want "something," even the satisfaction of a warm reunion with an opponent, and faith is often "nothing."

We know that peace-making is often first conflict-making. "If your brother or sister sins against you, go and tell them their fault, between you alone" (Matthew 18:15). That does not feel like reconciliation. In fact, it does not even feel "Christian," if that is what we are trying to feel.

Yes, the goal is union and reconciliation, but first of all the goal is nakedness. Nothing new can happen unless we can empty out the old. We cannot be clothed afresh without taking off the previous clothes. It has to do with self-image and our attachment to it. That insecure self-image will hide behind principles, the holding of moral claims and the protecting of great eternal truths. But usually these are all rags: "all that integrity of ours is like filthy clothing . . . " (Isaiah 64:5). Unless there is a willingness to be naked, to lessen our attachment to our offended or positive self-image, we cannot take the first steps toward reconciliation. We will sit around waiting and praying for the vindication of our own righteousness.

To risk conflict-making is to trust God's presence in our brother and sister. To risk sharing our truth with another is to admit that we probably do not have the whole truth or even the whole picture. Sometimes we find out, to our chagrin, that we do not even want it. It is much easier to live with our comforting self-image, to hold the moral high ground, than to take the low road where the Lamb of God walks hidden and "without beauty" (Isaiah 53:2).

The truth will set you *free*, but it will also set you *down*. Those unwilling to go down into their ashes will meet some other god, but they will not meet Jesus. He always enters the

holy city on a donkey. There he "made a whip of cords" (John
2:15). He chose and owned his anger so he could express it
with clarity and purpose. We often deny and disguise ours,
because it does not feel Christian. Then we hurt our brother
or sister indirectly or under a confused pretext. The evil or sin
cannot be named or forgiven because it hides in the shadows.

I remember my years as pastor of New Jerusalem, where it
usually seemed that the issue before us was never the real issue.
Control, ego, righteousness could never show themselves as
such in a Christian community—or they would be exorcised.
No, the "angels of darkness must disguise themselves as angels
of light" (1 Corinthians 11:14). Our angers were always holy
zeal for truth and purity. Or better yet, we were not "angry"
at all, just sullen and contentious!

If we can risk emptiness, our attachment to self-image, and
a healthy expression of our angers, true reconciliation is at least
possible. But there are some positive choices, too. We must
see forgiveness and union as the desire that God puts into the
hearts of his children. "Blessed are the peacemakers for they
shall be called the sons and daughters of God" (Matthew 5:9).
If we do not even desire to *desire*, then we have made friends
with darkness and the Spirit is not in us. "But this do we know
that we have passed from death to life, if we love the brethren.
If you refuse to love, you will remain dead; to hate your sister
is to be a murderer" (1 John 3:14-15). The Spirit within us
creates an unrelenting desire toward forgiveness and reconciliation. It must be acted on.

I am so convinced of this evidence of the presence of the
Spirit that I could even describe the whole gospel as the unfold-
ing mystery of forgiveness. Forgiveness is the beginning, the
middle, and the end of the gospel life. It is the energy of being
forgiven that first buoys us up. It is the experience of being
forgiven (when we didn't even think we needed it) that renews
our flagging spirit. It is profound forgiveness that becomes
God's providence and mercy at the end.

Zachariah spoke well when he said that God would "give his

people knowledge of salvation through forgiveness of sin" (Luke 1:77). It is as important to give it as it is to receive it. On both sides of the equation, you know you are enjoying a life and power not your own. Forgiveness given (which means it is unearned, undeserved, and unnecessary) and forgiveness received (unearned, undeserved, and unnecessary) are always the pure work of uncreated grace. It is the supreme work of God for the re-creation of all things.

Nothing new happens without forgiveness. We just keep repeating the same old patterns, illusions, and half-truths. Sometimes the grace does not come immediately, but like Job we "sit in the ashes scraping our sores" (Job 2:8). Sometimes neither the desire nor the decision to forgive is present. Then we must grieve and wait. We must sit in our poverty, perhaps even admitting our inability to forgive to the offender. That is when we learn how to pray and how to "long and thirst for righteousness" (Matthew 5:6).

I have seen far too much pseudo-forgiveness and quick reconciliation in Christian circles. It has the character of problem-solving and Yankee pragmatism instead of the patient and humble spirit of Jesus. It too quickly preserves my self-image as a magnanimous person instead of quietly walking the mystery of iniquity and healing. True Spirit-led forgiveness always frees and heals at least one of the parties involved, and hopefully both of them. If it only preserves our own moral high ground, I doubt if it is true forgiveness. It must also quicken and invite the hearts of others, especially the offender. I am sure we have all been "forgiven" by someone in a patronizing way that only binds us up all the more. The Spirit of Jesus will not do that. To paraphrase Paul, the forgiveness of Jesus is patient and kind, never boastful or conceited, never rude or selfish; it does not take offense, and is not resentful. True forgiveness takes no pleasure in other people's sins but delights in the truth; it is always ready to excuse, to trust, to hope, and to endure whatever comes (1 Corinthians 13:4-7).

At New Jerusalem in Cincinnati I had them paint "70 x 7"

over the main doorway. New mail carriers would always think
it was the address! It *was* our address, in a way. It is the dis-
tinctive hallmark of a people liberated by Christ. For Christian
community is not where forgiveness is unnecessary or
unneeded. Christian community is where forgiveness is free to
happen. And if it doesn't happen — on a daily basis — there will
be no Christian community.

OUT OF A PRAYERFUL HEART

An Interview with Richard Rohr

For the past five years you've been involved with the Center for Action and Contemplation — equal emphasis in that name on action and contemplation. How do those two activities work together in Christian living?

Those two words have become classic Catholic terminology for the two polarities of our lives. Thomas Aquinas said that the highest form of Christian life is not action or contemplation, but the ability to integrate the two. In religious life we were always told it was our task to bring the two together, to be active contemplatives or contemplative activists.

I am more convinced now than ever that the real art of Christian living is successfully to synthesize these two patterns, to bring them together in one life. It doesn't come without a lot of mistakes and practice and prayer. Invariably, too, as you go through life you swing on a pendulum between the two extremes. You'll look at a particular period in your life and say that time was obviously more active or more contemplative than another.

What I'm seeing today that somewhat alarms me is the tendency to call any kind of inner work contemplation. That isn't

or true. Inner work might lead you to a contemplative
t not necessarily. My concern is that we're almost at
the point of confusing any kind of inner work, insight-gathering
or introspection with spirituality. Spirituality is the work of
love, which is always somehow too the work of God. Spirituality
is about letting go of the false much more than collecting the
new, the therapeutic, or the helpful. The equation has become
this: to do inner stuff is to be spiritual — and that can't be true!
To be spiritual really is to be integrating history with our inner
life, to look at what's happening out there in the world first
and then look inside and put the two together in some pro-
ductive way. Otherwise, we're going to remain in that sacred-
secular split forever, always stuck in the notion that what it
means to be a spiritual person is to be an "inner" person,
whereas "secular" people are only concerned about the outer
world.

But that innerness too often is just narcissism or navel-gaz-
ing. It can be just highly self-serving ways of taking care of
yourself. Along with this selfishness can come an exalted self-
image of yourself as being a very spiritual person. This must
be what happens with those gurus who end up owning Cadillacs
and manipulating their followers.

Having said that, I want to point out the other side of the
problem, that the sin of our country probably lies on the other
side of the equation: too much activism without any inner work,
insight, or examination of conscience. We have seen it most
recently in the tragedy of the Persian Gulf war. It appears to
me that a large majority of our citizenry have done no inner
work, have no inner sense of integration, conscience, or integrity or they wouldn't be so easily led over the edge. The jin-
goism that was sold on the evening news was bought with hardly
any criticism. That came from being too active, too much in
the outer world, too much on the surface of things, it seems to
me.

I saw it again recently in the idolatrous victory celebrations
in New York City and Washington, D.C. Here we have cities

where the school system is falling apart, the homeless and hungry crowd the streets, yet overnight they could find millions of dollars to celebrate a military victory. That seems to me to be a gross and obscene example of the lack of interiority and integrity in the American people.

Our work, as Christians, is to put the two together—the inner and the outer, what's going on in the world and in history and what's going on inside our hearts, action and contemplation. To help people act effectively in the world out of an inner centeredness, out of a sense of God. That's our job.

Another big part of this effort to integrate the inner and the outer is the ability to look at both sides of life equally hard. We must be able to face the joy and wonder of life as well as the pain and injustice and absurdity. I call this dark side of life the left hand of God or the painful mystery of things. My recent encounter with cancer is a good example. I had been preaching about the painful mystery of things for many months, and then it reached out and grabbed me and got my attention.

That's how it happens. You're going along fine, things are going well, and then wham, you're struck by the left hand of God, you see the terrible pain and injustice and absurdity that is a part of everything, either in your own life or in the lives of those around you. Then, if you are open, you're driven back to an inner place so that you can try to make sense out of it all somehow. And, of course, no one can make sense out of it. One just learns to live with it gracefully. True action, effective Christian action, means looking hard at both sides of life, and that look will drive you back to your inner life, to the contemplative stance.

And that contemplative place, if it's God-centered, honest and whole, will drive you forward to a passion to do something about the pain of the world. If it doesn't lead to that passion (all the saints of the church have said this), then don't trust it. There's all this pain, and you want to do something about it. God will lead you to a place of solidarity and engagement, if you aim for this integration of action and contemplation. You can't just keep analyzing your dreams and digging deeper within yourself, learning more about your Myers-Briggs or Enneagram type.

We had over a hundred men meet together in the mountains here two weeks ago for a men's gathering. I told them that I could help them to get in touch with their feelings. God knows we men need to get in touch with our feelings in this society, and thank God many are making the effort. But past a certain level, so what? What are you going to do with those feelings? Where are those feelings going to lead you? You have to do something in the real world, not just indulge or feel your feelings all day long. That's what we're trying to do at the Center for Action and Contemplation. We want to help people integrate these two ends of the pendulum swing so that we can all move toward a better world, one that is more whole and life-giving for all. None of us has achieved it in our own lives completely, but we're all working toward that goal. When the body with its emotions, the soul with its inner life, and the spirit with its God-center all connect, then we must act. That is the biblical and transformative pattern.

In your talks and tapes, you continue to emphasize the importance of a solid connection with the poor, the marginalized, the outcasts in our society. Why is that connection so important for you?

I feel that the outer poverty, injustice, and absurdity we see when we look around us mirrors our own inner poverty, injustice, and absurdity. The poor man or woman outside is an invitation to the poor man or woman inside. As you learn compassion and sympathy for the brokenness of things, when you encounter the visible icon of the painful mystery in "the little ones," then, if you have built bridges between the inner and outer, if you have learned to move between action and contemplation, then you'll learn compassion and sympathy for the "little one," the brokenness within yourself. You'll realize that you are a poor person too. You are full of pain and negativity, and there's nothing you can do about it right now.

Recovering from surgery now, I have to sit home with my own broken absurdity as much as I had to sit with it at the soup kitchen a while back. The poor man's poverty at the soup kitchen is visible and extraverted; mine is invisible and interior, but just as real. So the two sympathies and compassion connect and it becomes one world. I think that's why Jesus said we have to recognize Christ in the least of our brothers and sisters. It was for *our* redemption, *our* liberation, *our* healing. When we see it over there, we become freed in here, and we also become less judgmental. I can't hate the person on welfare because I realize I'm on God's welfare. It all becomes one truth, and the inner and the outer reflect one another.

As compassion and sympathy flow out of us to the poor, to the outcast, wounds are bandaged—both others' and our own. We'll never bandage them all, nor do we need to, but we do need to get close to the wounds. That idea is imaged so well in the gospels with Thomas, the doubting apostle. He wants to figure things out in his head. He's done too much inner work, too much analyzing and explaining. He always needs more data before he can move. Then Jesus tells him he must put his finger inside the wounds. Then and only then does he begin to understand what faith is all about.

Thomas, I think, is an archetype of too much of our church's history. The church has tried to resolve all theological dilemmas with analysis and academic thinking. It just doesn't work. It produces a faith that isn't real, that has no passion in it, no reality, no power to compel—just endless theological distinctions and books and articles while the world goes by and says, who cares? This wouldn't have happened if we'd kept Jesus' counsel to stay close to the poor. The poor kept us close to the gospels, to the important questions and issues, to the Christ-child within and without.

In many ways, I think we have become a Leviticus church more than an Exodus church. When the clergy and ceremony take over and fail to keep that solidarity with the poor, then the Book of Leviticus takes over. We become overly concerned with laws and liturgies, structure, ceremony and vestment, with what goes on inside the church building. But most church doesn't happen best inside of the church.

The Exodus church, on the other hand, is the church in touch with the poor, hearing their cry. It is the church on a journey, busy encountering history, the outer world, liberation from slavery, the church as lifestyle and action, meeting along the way a much more gutsy God than that of the Leviticus church. I'm very fortunate in that my travels often take me out to that Exodus church. I meet wonderful Catholics who are out in the trenches listening to the poor. They've been formed by the tradition and they know what they know and love what they love, and are living it out. It's encouraging to see more and more of this kind of church. However, I do believe and accept that it will always be a remnant, a minority—just as in Exodus.

In this art of bringing action and contemplation together, what is the hardest part for you?

Getting myself out of the way, I suppose, is the most difficult part. It's conversion process, and conversion means self-surrender, letting go of control, trusting. That's difficult for all of us. For example, you can't set out to surrender. If you take it on as a project, then it becomes an ego adventure and leads nowhere. It's another way to exercise your spiritual muscles and then you're back in control again in the name of being surrendered to God's will.

It's very tricky, this surrender business. It's not something you do, it's done to you, it's drawn forth from you. The New Testament names it so well where John (21:18f) talks about the first half of life wherein you do what you want to do, go where you want to go. Then, in the second half of life, another will come and put a belt around you and take you where you would rather not go. Surrender is the language of the second half of life. In the first half, we have to increase so that Christ can increase. The second part of life holds forth the task of

John the Baptist, or what we hear at the end of John's gospel. In the second half of life, I must decrease so Christ can increase. It's the way of John the Baptist, and it probably won't feel much like self-actualization.

Often, we give people in the first half of life this task of the second half. You can't tell a twenty-year-old kid about surrender unless that kid has been really well loved and has built a strong container for his own ego and personality. He will turn sacrificial language into disguised self-actualization. I'm afraid that's what happened to many young, idealistic seminarians and religious in our church.

If you are on the path, living out the journey with integrity and honesty, then there comes a point (usually about the mid-thirties or early forties) when you realize that you've got to start letting go, that you're trying to control reality and life too much. You are used to your patterns, you know what you can make happen from past experiences. So you end up pushing people around and manipulating events, and pretty soon God is no longer in charge. You are in charge every step of the way, making sure you feel the feelings you want to feel and never have to face any discomfort or pain you don't want to face.

I see that in my own life all the time. I'm always organizing my life around my own definition of holiness. But holiness can never be defined. What is it? I think we can only know it by its effects. There is a certain kind of freedom, vitality, simplicity, courage, humor, and spontaneity that others experience in the presence of holiness. It's like the electron we learn about in modern physics. No instrument can see it or measure it; we can only deduce what it's like by watching its effects on everything else.

There are many kinds of holiness. We're too much in the grip of an institutional definition of holiness. I was told as a young man about St. Aloysius who always kept his head down whenever he was confronted by a beautiful woman. That's not holiness; that's just weird. Why would God create the beautiful human form and then ask us not to look at it? A holy man would have to be one who looks at that beauty and says, yes, that delights me. God made that for delight. It doesn't mean I have to possess it, lust after it, but I can surely enjoy it and let it be. That's integration, that's wholeness.

The church has too often defined holiness as subservience and obedience because that's the kind of person those in power want around them so they can stay in power. To those on top, the person who does what they say is defined as the holy one. But isn't that a bit self-serving? If you're a parent with two kids, a wild one and an obedient one, which one will you call the good child? Probably the obedient one, because it's easier to run a household with that one. But who knows how these kids will turn out in the long run? It could be that the one who is the most rebellious, who thought for herself, asked you a thousand questions you couldn't answer and got into more trouble is the one who later in life does the most for the world and grows up the healthiest.

I believe profoundly in surrender, but I don't think we can chart its course ahead of time. Surrender is something that is done to us. I've been studying Joseph Campbell's books on the hero's journey in myth and story. He says that the only way to be a hero is to prepare and *be ready* when the moment comes. You can't pick ahead of time which dragon you'll slay. The opportunity always sneaks up on you, and then all you can do is *be ready*. The teachings of Jesus are very clear on this: When the crisis comes you must know how to respond courageously and with conscience so you'll do the heroic thing. This gets us back to the recent tragic war.

It has been a very sobering experience for me to experience how unready we all were for it. When the big crisis came, most of us weren't prepared. Jesus told us that it comes like a thief in the night. He wasn't just talking about death and the afterlife. He was talking about the crises that demand our right action, our purposeful witness rooted in conviction and integrity. Suddenly there was this huge, manipulated event looming, and the souls of most of us were not ready to see through the deceit, the illusion, the self-serving rhetoric that was going on. We hung out our ribbons and waved our flags and the gospel went out the window and tens of thousands of Iraqis died. The day before the war started, 80 percent, according to the polls, disapproved. The day after the war started, 80 percent, according to the same polls, were behind it. What that tells me about our country, our church, is very saddening.

How do you ready yourself for these moments of crisis?

I think you get ready by getting yourself out of the way. All the great spiritual disciplines of the world point to this. You ready yourself for heroic and holy action by not taking yourself and your needs and wants too seriously, by not giving your feelings, your securities, your preoccupations the highest priority. Isn't that what praying, fasting, and almsgiving (the three classic disciplines in Christian spirituality) are all about? When we pray, fast, and give alms, we're saying that I'm not the center of the world. God is the center, not me. If you lose sight of this discipline, you lose the ability to see clearly. Everything is filtered through the prism of self and the self's need to be liked and approved of.

Most of the people who jumped on the bandwagon for the war are good people. And it seemed that what happened was that everyone wanted to feel good about themselves, feel good about what we were doing, feel good about the troops over there, so, as a result, all questions of morality and conscience went out the window. No one wanted to face the pain, the uncertainty, the difficult weighing of pros and cons that was necessary to act with conscience. We just all wanted to feel good about America and our part in it.

Come on! For me, that's avoidance of the paschal mystery. At the middle of our eucharist, we stop and proclaim the mystery of our faith. Not a mystery, but *the* mystery. "Christ has died, Christ has risen, Christ will come again." That's it. The paschal mystery. In the East, they call this the yin and yang of things. If you're Jungian, you call it the darkness and the light.

It's a statement about the mystery of life: that half of life is full of death, pain, it's unjust, absurd, dishonest, doesn't work, requires hard choices and arduous effort. That's "Christ has died." And the other side of the mystery is that half of life is full of joy, beauty, humor, love. That's "Christ is risen."

Just recently I found a cancerous mole on my leg. The first prognosis was two to six months to live. "Christ died." After the surgery, my house looked like a florist shop as many of my friends and relatives showed me the unconditional love they feel for me. "Christ is risen." It would take the rest of my life to enjoy and savor the love I've been shown in the past few weeks. Always, always in life, there's this paschal mystery, there's joy and pain interwoven, richness and poverty, darkness and light, all together.

The mystery of our faith is the paschal mystery. The church has to proclaim this strongly and consistently, now more loudly than ever. We've got to ask ourselves what this paschal mystery means in terms of today, right now, right in the middle of our living, what it means in terms of the events on the nightly news. Otherwise, as time goes on, more catastrophes like the Persian Gulf war will swallow up our conscience and integrity as Christians. The stakes are global now. And, at issue, is the very credibility of the gospel.

A big problem for me and for others, I know, is this: We make some progress in the struggle you're describing, this integration of outer and inner work, then we rest on our laurels and look around us. And we feel we're better than everyone else. How do you avoid self-righteousness?

Whatever abuses you see in the outer world, if you can see them that means you've probably already recognized them in yourself and are aware of your own continuing capacity for evil. If you don't see the sin in yourself, then you probably can't describe it outside. The second difficult challenge is trying to love the people who don't agree with you and don't join your side right away. You can't immediately write off everyone who doesn't agree with you as a pagan, an atheist, or a rightwing warmonger. Those people are on a journey, on a path also. God has led you to this moment of recognition. You haven't perfectly put it together either.

This is hard. On the one hand we can't be naive about evil. We have to name it when we see it — in ourselves and in others. But we must not immediately damn the other side as totally without merit or conscience. We must not compartmentalize evil neatly into one group or person over there and then give ourselves permission to disdain them. All of us are looking for the moral high ground. I see people doing it with diets, with the environment, with social justice issues. We hate the old church for being so dogmatic and authoritarian, but woe unto you if you are caught eating a piece of red meat or not recycling an aluminum can. These actions now can be considered as sinful as fornication was a generation ago.

I struggle with the church about this, while at the same time I see it in myself all the time. We don't want to create new excuses for self-righteousness, for arrogance and false superiority. I find that as I get older this whole process takes on ever more subtle forms. It's another means of domination and control, another form of totalitarianism, and another way of not letting go of control. We can't trust our belief that God is at work in others' lives as well as our own.

The church, for me, is a statement of where human history is right now, how grace is encountering human history at this point. The church, in many ways, reflects what we can't see yet and what we are beginning to see. It's always a few steps behind the Spirit and it legitimizes what the Spirit has already helped us discover. It comes along and watches what happens, then proclaims: Yes, God is against racism. Yes, God is against sexism. Yes, God is against killing. Yes, God loves all of creation: the plants, the animals, the Earth herself. Peter is always late running to the tomb, but *he does* get there!

I see the paschal mystery, the darkness and light of things, square in the middle of the church. On the one hand, the church is the glorious face of Christ. On the other, it's the

Whore of Babylon, totally unfaithful to Christ. It pretends to be absolutely certain about birth control or married or women priests (about which Jesus said nothing), yet it has comfortable doubts about nonviolence, about riches and wealth (about which Jesus was *absolutely clear*).

What concerns me most are the young kids coming up with so little sense of where to find the sacred in their lives, where to find identity, guidance, and boundaries. I reflect on my own life and see that, even with everything going for me, with a rich formation and education in prayer and spirituality, it has still taken me forty-eight years to begin to come to some kind of honest and real appreciation of spiritual work. What about the eighteen-year-old confused, bewildered kid from Akron, Ohio? Who's going to teach him, guide him? That's what drives me to preach and make tapes and books. Where are the young of our society going to get their faith from? Faith is an elusive thing.

In my own talks, one of my favorite lines is this: Faith is giving away what you do not yet have. That's why it's faith; it operates partly out of complete blindness. Here, I'd like to speak in favor of our Catholic tradition. Catholicism, out of its 2,000-year experience, has accumulated a lot of wisdom about darkness, about the painful side of the paschal mystery. The desert fathers, the mystics, the saints, the founders of religious orders, all were people who had tasted enough light that they could risk the darkness. Nowadays faith has come to mean holding onto answers, finding certitude, having clarity about things, being sure we're absolutely right before we move on or take a risk. It's all concerned with "light" and fear of its counterpart.

But a look at our tradition will show that faith is really the opposite of certitude. Rather, it is being willing to move into darkness, into *not* being sure. It means taking risks, allowing ourselves to be taken advantage of, having the grace to move through chancy, uncertain waters, letting go of control and trusting that God will always be there. It means living with the mystery of things, not knowing for sure what's going to happen or that it'll turn out okay.

Here again, the inner and the outer reflect one another. Many of us personally are coming to this realization of what faith is. At the same time, in the outer world, the whole philosophy of modernism appears to be dying. What I call modernism is this recent faith in progress, a belief that human reason alone can solve all our problems, that technology will save us from the messes it has created. Everything is getting better and better, "GE Brings Good Things to Life," "Progress Is Our Most Important Product." All that is going down the tubes.

In its place, there seems to be coming the postmodern era. Here you see an appreciation of the nonrational once again, interest in the occult, the intuitive, spiritual — the New Age. You see it in the men's movement, in the drumming and chanting. There's a different way of knowing, another way besides human reason to find direction and guidance. My hope is that we'll discover new levels of biblical faith, a new opening into our Christian tradition of wisdom, which balances the nonrational with the rational. Reason alone has failed us utterly. The whole planet is being destroyed by college-educated people.

How do you find yourself praying these days?

I feel as though I've just had direct experience in my body of the two hands of God, both the left hand, the painful mystery, and the right hand, the warm generous lover who gives me everything I need. My prayer is showing me that finally I am beginning to be able to trust those two hands of God. When I was facing the big issues and whether I really believed in the resurrection I've been preaching all my life, I noticed that God was always with me, there was always this connection. I couldn't have kicked God out of the room. The issues were too big and vital. It gives me great hope for that prayer I said when I was a kid, that "now *and* at the hour of our death." The Hail Mary worked!

When I looked back over my life, I saw the two hands of God leading me to where I am right now, walking with me always, never leaving my side. At the time I may not have seen it, but looking back I did. Now by the grace of God I believe I can trust the future because those hands have upheld me so well in my past.

I find that I need a lot of solitude these days. I'm an extrovert, but there is just too much pain, too much injustice crying out, too much nonsensical reality coming at me. Only silence and solitude are broad enough and deep enough to absorb the contradictions. Not words, not explanations in books, not theology, not my own tapes and books, only silence is enough. I feel that if I'm going to be talking and preaching about faith and the scriptures as if I know what I'm talking about, then I have to keep cleaning the lens. I've got to keep getting myself out of the way to make sure I'm preaching God's agenda and not my own. I want to always be preaching out of a prayerful heart. So silence and solitude are job requirements for me.

When I clean the lens, a clarity comes that allows me to live without anger, anxiety, or cynicism. Sometimes cynicism seems the easiest response to the painful mystery. It's clever and makes you sound intelligent, but it's not the spirit of Jesus. His spirit is more patient, trusting, ready to find humor and beauty in the middle of things and enjoy them. Right in the middle of all the pain, injustice, and absurdity of the paschal mystery, there's always this: "Christ is risen." I can't doubt or deny that power anymore.